ILLUSTRATING COMPUTERS

Colin Day read natural sciences at
Cambridge, expecting to end up doing research in
physics. Instead he found himself turned around
and sent off to Vietnam to do three years of
linguistic research and Bible translation. A three year
Ph.D. course in general linguistics followed (in
London), trying to sort out the grammar of a
minor language of Vietnam. It was then that he
discovered how computers can help reduce the
drudgery of sifting through large quantities of
information. A year or so in India and Nepal
provided an opportunity to produce dictionaries
by means of a computer in Bombay. Since 1967
he has been working in the Computer Centre at
University College London, writing computer
programs to handle letters and words rather than
numbers.

Donald Alcock read engineering at Cambridge,
then designed bridges in Africa and Canada. In
1957 he realised a computer could do bridge
calculations quicker than he could, so went to an
American university to learn how. He became an
assistant professor of civil engineering but saw
no future in teaching without a Ph.D. — and had
not the wit or stamina at age thirty to go for
one. Instead he joined Ferranti Limited and wrote
engineering programs for antique computers (then
shiny new) with names like Pegasus, Sirius and
Atlas. Five years later he became founding
partner of a technical computer consultancy — a
firm that lasted fifteen years. He has now
retired from the technical software business to
see more of his family and write books and
things.

COLIN DAY
DONALD ALCOCK

ILLUSTRATING COMPUTERS
(WITHOUT MUCH JARGON)

Pan Books   London and Sydney
in association with   Heinemann Computers in Education

First published 1982 by Pan Books Ltd,
Cavaye Place, London SW10 9PG
in association with Heinemann Computers in Education,
22 Bedford Square, London WC1B 3HH

ISBN 0 330 26599 7

Printed and bound in Great Britain by
Richard Clay (The Chaucer Press) Ltd, Bungay, Suffolk

1 WHY BOTHER ABOUT THEM?
(THE IMPORTANCE OF COMPUTERS)

Why bother about computers? Why not leave them to the elite who understand them?

You cannot dismiss computers as easily as that. Their influence is spreading rapidly through our society. From supermarket checkout counters to the corridors of power their influence is felt. Most bills are now prepared by computers — so are wage slips. But computers are involved in less obvious areas. They may control traffic lights throughout town and the local telephone exchange. They may have controlled the construction of your car. The special effects in the latest space movie may have been produced by means of computers. There may even be a few tiny 'computers' about the home.

Why is it that computers are in such widespread use? This is mainly because of an enormous reduction in both the cost and the size of computers – coupled with their increasing power and flexibility. As a result the number of computers has increased and is increasing ever more rapidly.

The first completely electronic calculator (not *quite* a computer) was developed at the University of Pennsylvania in 1945 and was called ENIAC. By 1950 there were in the world 15 computers completed or being built. Thirty years on, the Computer Users' Yearbook for 1980 lists a total of 26,872 computers in the United Kingdom and Eire alone. However, this figure is for medium to large installations; the number of small computers must be far greater. Including the smallest – the 'microcomputers' – the total for the whole world must run to many millions.

It is now possible to buy a microcomputer at about the same price as a black and white television receiver. Such a microcomputer does arithmetic twenty times faster than ENIAC did, it has a larger memory and is thousands of times more reliable. It consumes the same power as an electric light bulb, whereas ENIAC needed enough power to drive a locomotive. ENIAC took up 30,000 times the space and cost 10,000 times as much as today's microcomputer.

DRIVING POWER c.1945

DRIVING POWER c.1981

CONTENTS

Preface

1 Why bother about them ?   1
  (The importance of computers)

2 What are they like ?   6
  (Overall characteristics)

3 What is inside them ?   11
  (Representation of information)

4 How do they work ?   18
  (Machine instructions)

5 How do they do it ?   25
  (Hardware operations)

6 Where do chips come in ?   32
  (Microelectronics)

7 What can you plug in ?   42
  (Peripheral devices)

8 What do they understand ?   50
  (Programming languages)

9 How do you program them ?   56
  (Programming)

10 Who looks after them ?   65
  (Operating systems)

11 What use are they ?   72
  (Applications)

12 What is a micro ?   81
  (Microcomputers)

13 Where will it all lead ?   92
  (Future developments)

Index   101

To our wives and
families for all the
help they gave us.

PREFACE

This book is for those who want to know something about computers but have so far been put off by the jargon. The principles underlying computers are simple, however, and these we have tried to illustrate without assuming any previous knowledge of the subject.

Illustrating computers may be compared to sketching a building from a few essential vantage points. The sketches do not pick out every surface detail, nor do they illustrate the complete shape of the building, but they give a clear impression of it. The artist should not select unusual vantage points nor give a false sense of proportion by exaggerating perspective. The sketches in this book are intended to give a true impression for the layman to read. They are not for the computer expert — the already initiated — who would find deficiencies in our explanations and exceptions to our generalizations.

We wanted to give a bibliography for further reading but found it impossible to compile. It all depends which way the reader wants to go when finished with this book. The next step could be to visit a computer hobby shop — browse among books on the computer shelves of a book shop — subscribe to one of the glossy computer magazines — enroll on a course in computer science — seek an interview for a job with a computer company...

Read this book first.

Because computers are rapidly getting cheaper and more easily available they are widely used, valued, respected — even feared. Computers work rapidly, tirelessly, obediently and (contrary to folklore) almost never make mistakes. They can do many things which have up to now been done by people. They can enable one person to do a task which used to take a dozen or more people (or would not be contemplated at all because of the labour involved). Some fear the widespread use of computers may cause more and more unemployment. There is all the more reason, therefore, for knowing what computers are like and what they can do. Only then may any potential threat be assessed objectively.

It is not necessary to understand the workings of a television receiver before switching it on. Likewise it is not necessary to know how a computer works in order to use one. This book explains the workings of a computer for two reasons: Firstly, people who may never have to operate a computer or write a computer program would nevertheless like to know how a bundle of electronic components can do what it is reported to do. Secondly, in order to appreciate the revolution these machines are causing it is as well to know something of how they are made and how they function. Only with this knowledge can one judge both the potential of computers and their limitations. Any mystery surrounding computers can be dispelled only by giving some explanation of the way they go about their work.

Computers are very different from everything else we know. It is hard to relate them to other things of which we have experience. Chapter 2 describes the major types of computer and gives some analogies to help show what a computer is *like*.

One aspect which makes computers unique is their ability to process information. That information is represented inside the computer using only the two <u>numeric digits 0 and 1</u>. This is not as limiting as it might seem. Chapter 3 shows how various types of information may be stored within a computer.

Instructions are also coded as 0's and 1's and stored in the computer's memory. Chapter 4 describes how such instructions are obeyed in sequence as a *program*.

It is hard to imagine how electronics can perform arithmetic such as adding two numbers. Chapter 5 provides a non-technical description of how this can be done.

The reduction in cost and size of computers has come about by the development of the *silicon chip* whose manufacture is revealed in Chapter 6.

If a computer is an 'electronic brain' it needs hands, eyes, ears and mouth to be able to respond. Chapter 7 reviews some of the devices that may be plugged into a computer as the equivalent of limbs to an animal.

If the instructions a computer has to obey are all strings of 0's and 1's one might suppose communication with the machine would be extremely difficult. As Chapter 8 shows, computers can be made to understand other languages besides their own.

In order to give some idea of what it is like to write a program for a computer, Chapter 9 gives an example of a program written in one of the most common programming languages.

As computers have grown in size and complexity they have been given more responsibility for controlling their own work. The development of special programs called *operating systems* is sketched in Chapter 10.

The uses to which computers have been applied are so varied and numerous that Chapter 11 can give only a few examples to indicate areas in which computers are making their presence felt.

Although it is true that microcomputers differ from large machines in terms of size and cost (rather than any fundamental way of working) they are becoming so cheap and small that they may be used in ways never contemplated for their bigger cousins. Chapter 12 has therefore been specially devoted to 'micros'.

Everyone would like to know what lies ahead. The authors claim no prophetic foresight. In Chapter 13 we indicate some possible developments of this rapidly changing technology.

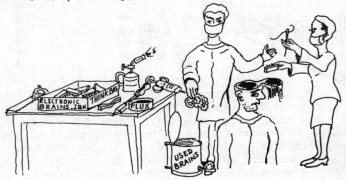

2 WHAT ARE THEY LIKE ?
(OVERALL CHARACTERISTICS)

The problem faced by most people when hearing about computers is to get a rough idea of *what they are like*. When we encounter a new machine we try to relate it to things we already know, giving it a place within our knowledge of the world. The difficulty with computers is that they are so different from everything else. In one sense they are like nothing else on Earth.

The physical appearance of computers is little or no help towards understanding them. Computers are mostly boxes with nothing much appearing to happen to them. When confronted with several boxes and other bits and pieces it's puzzling to know which one *is* the computer.

Seeing several computers is even more bewildering because they can look so different. Some fill a large room with their various boxes. Others may be desk-sized and perhaps desk-shaped. (This is roughly the kind called a *mini-computer*.) Yet other devices are the size of a typewriter. (These are commonly termed *microcomputers* or just *micros*.) So the physical appearance is not much help to people wanting to know what a computer is like.

large main frame

The computer has been described as an 'electronic brain', but this can be misleading. Both the computer and the human brain can store information in a memory and process that information (by arithmetic for instance). But the way they do these things appears to be very different. A computer memorizes and recalls information almost instantaneously whereas the brain may take a number of repetitions to memorize. Recalling something may be agonizing for a human and may take several minutes. On the other hand...

Recognizing distorted LETTERING

... is a simple and rapid task for the brain compared with a computer.

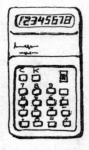

Perhaps the closest piece of equipment to a computer is a calculator. Indeed some calculators are so sophisticated they might be classed as computers. Silicon chips are used in their manufacture (as described in Chapter 6). Numbers may be fed in and stored. Arithmetic may be performed on those numbers. The result may be displayed. All these things are true of both computers and calculators.

Even this analogy is inadequate. A computer is not confined to processing numbers. It can also handle letters, words and diagrams. But even more important, a computer does not have to wait for a human being to tap keys before doing each arithmetical (or other) operation.

There are various classes of computer not described in this book. The type described here is technically known as a *general purpose digital computer* and is the most common kind. Some explanation is needed for the terms *general purpose* and *digital*.

A musical box which only plays 'Pop goes the weasel' is a special-purpose device. When you are in the mood for hearing 'Pop goes the weasel' this musical box comes into its own; otherwise it is not much use. If, on the other hand, it is the kind of musical box where you can replace the spiked cylinder to make it play other tunes it becomes a more general-purpose device.

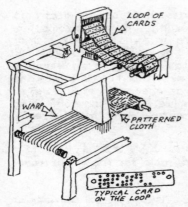

LOOP OF CARDS

WARP

PATTERNED CLOTH

TYPICAL CARD ON THE LOOP

An ordinary loom is special-purpose. It can weave cloth only in the usual under-and-over kind of way. A Jacquard loom is different. It has a loop of cards with holes punched in them. Each card in turn comes against a set of needles. Wherever there is a hole in the card a needle falls through – and this causes a corresponding thread of the warp to be lifted. The pattern of holes in the loop of cards thus determines the pattern on the emerging cloth. A Jacquard loom is therefore general-purpose.

In the examples of a musical box and a loom the machine is general purpose if you can change the set of instructions (the spiked cylinder or loop of cards). Computers are _general purpose_ if one can _change_ the set of instructions – the _program_. Computers have shown themselves to be so useful simply because programs can be written to do such different things. The question, 'Can a computer do it?' is almost exactly the same as asking, 'Can you write a program to do it?'

General-purpose computers would not be able to do anything unless people had written programs for them. The clever things computers do (such as correctly calculating a mid-course correction for a spacecraft) are the result of programs written by people called _programmers_. The foolish things computers do (such as paying salaries of a million pounds or sending out electricity bills for zero amounts) have the same origin.

Digital is the opposite of _analogue_. Watches can be digital (with, say, a liquid crystal display) or analogue (with hands sweeping round). The difference is that a digital watch shows the time as a series of digits, and the number of possible times it can show is limited. The time shown varies from, say, 3:45:07 to 3:45:08 without visibly going through intermediate forms. On an analogue watch the time is infinitely variable. If you were to take photographs of the dial you would find it impossible to get two shots exactly alike unless the watch had stopped.

There are analogue computers that represent information (numbers) by means of continuously varying voltages. However, almost all computers are similar to the digital watch in the sense that they represent information as a series of digits. At each position on the face of a digital watch there is a limited number of digits that can be displayed. This is at the most the ten digits 0 to 9. Numbers written using these ten digits are called *decimal numbers*. These are the numbers familiar to everyone.

Digital computers almost without exception do not use decimal numbers for their internal working. Instead they use only the two digits 0 and 1. Numbers written using only these two digits are called *binary numbers*.

The reason for digital computers using the binary system is that it is the simplest way to store and process information. The distinction between a 0 and a 1 may be represented by a switch that is either on or off, part of a circuit that is conducting or not conducting, a wire that has a positive or zero voltage, a piece of iron magnetized one way or the other and so on. Cards for a Jacquard loom may be considered to be coded in binary because the important point is whether, at a particular place on a card, there is or is not a hole. When there are only two possibilities each can be represented very simply.

Such a rudimentary system does not limit the information that can be stored in a computer. As the next chapter shows, it is possible to represent decimal numbers, letters or words quite easily as binary numbers.

Although the computer finds it easiest to work in binary the people who *use* computers are not expected to use binary numbers. Information fed into a computer —or produced as output — may be in forms with which we are more familiar (for example decimal numbers). The computer performs the translation to and from binary as required.

To summarize: a computer takes information in binary form, processes the information in accordance with a set of instructions called a program, and produces output. The processing includes arithmetic, copying information from one place to another, and performing comparisons. By carrying out a large number of tiny operations the overall effect is achieved.

PROGRAM
* TAKE A NUMBER
* HALVE IT
* SQUARE THE RESULT
* MULTIPLY BY π
* PRINT THE ANSWER

5·3

0101
0101
0110
0101

Indefatigable
Computer
Laundries

22·1

3 WHAT IS INSIDE THEM?
(REPRESENTATION OF INFORMATION)

If you open up a computer you see a mass of wires, circuit boards and electronic components. This chapter does not deal with the circuitry, however, but with the *information* inside the computer. In the last chapter it was said that information is stored and processed using the binary system. The data which computers are required to process are rarely in the form of 1's and 0's to begin with. The data may consist of names and addresses, amounts of money owing, numbers of parts ordered and so on. If the computer is to handle such information it must be *coded* in binary form.

A code is not just something used by secret agents. Coding may be used to change information into a more manageable form. For example in the early days of the telegraph, words were transmitted by means of the code devised by Samuel Morse.

Information may be coded in a variety of ways but the result is not always easy to process. It would be possible, for example, to take the score of a Beethoven symphony, describe each note in words, then transmit the words to instrumentalists using the Semaphore code. The information is there, but the orchestra might find it difficult to process.

Numbers can be coded using the Romans' method but in that form they are not easy to multiply.

(Perhaps this is the reason the Romans were not great mathematicians. But they did use computers — bead frames — for financial calculations.)

Computers can store and process information most easily if it is coded in the binary system. In other words only the digits 0 and 1 are used. A *binary digit* (0 or 1) is referred to so often there is a shortened name for it — *a bit.*
For years the favourite way of storing bits in the computer involved tiny rings of magnetic material (*cores*). These represent a 1 when magnetized in one direction and a 0 in the other. Wires through the rings switch the magnetization and test its direction.

These days core stores have been overtaken by many tiny electronic circuits, each one representing a 1 when conducting and a 0 when not.

Bits are not only stored by means of electronics —they are also readily *processed*. Chapter 5 shows how circuits may be used to add together two binary numbers.

The consequence of all this is that information fed into a computer must be translated into binary numbers. Because we are most familiar with the decimal system some explanation of binary numbers is needed.

You might think that numbers coded as 0's and 1's would be more limited than numbers coded using all ten digits. This is not so. Any number that can be represented using all ten digits can also be represented using only the two. To see how this works it is first necessary to be quite clear how to count using all *ten* digits.

Take the case of a mileometer on a bicycle. Each of the little wheels inside has the ten digits on it. As the bicycle goes from no miles to nine miles there is no problem in knowing how far you have come:

If the bicycle goes one mile more there is a difficulty. There is no digit for *ten*. Of course we all know what to do but seldom think what it implies. Set the last digit to zero and <u>carry</u> one. The resulting number says 'One group of ten and no units'. In general the columns may be labelled as shown below.

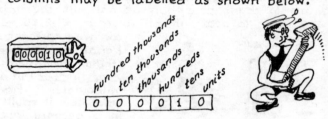

hundred thousands	ten thousands	thousands	hundreds	tens	units
0	0	0	0	1	0

There is then no difficulty in understanding that, for instance, the number 025708 means 'two ten thousands, five thousands, seven hundreds, no tens, and eight units'.

Now suppose we have a mileometer with only two digits on each wheel; 0 and 1. As the bicycle goes from no miles to one mile there is no problem: It is when the bicycle goes one more mile that the problem arises because there is no digit for *two*. So set the last digit to zero and *carry* one. This means 'one group of two and no units'. In general the columns may be labelled as shown below. As an example, the number 010110 in binary means 'one sixteen, no eights, one four, one two, and no units'; in other words 22.

thirty twos	sixteens	eights	fours	twos	units
0	0	0	0	1	0

In the memory store of a computer there are boxes which behave like binary mileometers. Each box can hold a row of bits. Positive whole numbers (0, 1, 2, 3, ...) can be held in such a binary mileometer as shown on the previous page. Negative whole numbers (-1, -2, -3, ...) could be represented by reserving the leftmost bit for the sign: 0 meaning positive and 1 meaning negative. (Computers differ in the way they represent negative numbers; this explanation shows one way of representing them.)

$$\boxed{0\,|\,0\,0\,|\,1\,0\,|\,1\,1\,0} \Rightarrow +22$$

$$'SIGN\ BIT' \Rightarrow \boxed{1\,|\,0\,0\,|\,1\,0\,|\,1\,1\,0} \Rightarrow -22$$

Up to now we have spoken only of storing whole numbers (or *integers* as mathematicians call them). This may suit the experimental farmer who wants to count peas but will not suit the statistician who needs to deal with an average of 2.65 people. How

can we represent a fractional number like this (the mathematical term is *real number*) in a binary mileometer? First consider how it could be done in a decimal mileometer.

Astronomers may need to use enormous numbers; microbiologists extremely small ones. Mathematicians have a way of making very large or small numbers easy to write. They would write the number 26,500,000,000 as $.265 \times 10^{11}$ (read as 'point two six five times ten to the eleventh') and 0.0000000265 they could write as $.265 \times 10^{-7}$. To do this they move the decimal point a number of places so as to get the fraction to a convenient position, then write the number of places they have moved the decimal point (11 meaning eleven places to the left; -7 meaning seven places to the right).

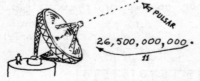

26,500,000,000 .
11

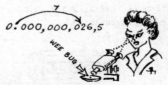

$$0.\overset{7}{\frown}000,000,026,5$$

Because space is limited in a mileometer the same trick could be used to make numbers more compact. Each real number has to be changed so that the decimal point comes before the first digit. The number of places that the decimal point has to be moved must be counted.

281.3 ⇨ .2813 on shifting *left* 3 places
0.0052 ⇨ .52 on shifting *right* 2 places

Now there are *two* numbers to pack into the mileometer; the fraction (.2813 or .52 here) and the shift for the decimal point (+3 or -2 here). The fact that the shift may be negative is awkward. As we are inventing the rules let us add 50 to every shift so as to make the number always (within practical limits) positive. The shifts here of +3 and -2 then become 53 and 48.

Now the two numbers can be put into decimal mileometers. They look like this:

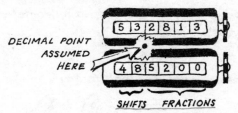

DECIMAL POINT
ASSUMED
HERE

SHIFTS   FRACTIONS

The shift occupies the first two places. The fraction goes in the rest of the mileometer. A decimal point cannot, of course, be shown in the mileometer because none of the wheels has one. So it has to be *assumed* that the decimal point comes immediately before the fraction.

A similar technique can be used for binary mileometers. A few bits can be used to keep the shift (usually called the *exponent*), and the rest of the mileometer used for the binary fraction. For example:

EXPONENT   SIGN BIT   BINARY FRACTION

| 1 1 0 1 0 0 0 1 | 1 | 1 1 0 1 0 0 1 1 1 0 0 1 0 1 1 1 0 0 1 0 0 1 0 |

It may be no surprise to hear that computers can store numbers. Some have the idea that computers are simply big calculating machines which can only manipulate numbers. This is just not true. Letters, words and sentences may also be stored and processed by computer. That means they must be coded in terms of 0's and 1's. To see how this is done the decimal mileometer may again be used as an analogy.

If a pair of digits is used to represent a letter of the alphabet, three letters would fit in one six-digit mileometer. A scheme could be invented for coding all twenty six letters as pairs of decimal digits. Here is a possible code:

A	00	F	05	K	10	P	15	U	20	Z	25
B	01	G	06	L	11	Q	16	V	21		
C	02	H	07	M	12	R	17	W	22		
D	03	I	08	N	13	S	18	X	23		
E	04	J	09	O	14	T	19	Y	24		

Now it is possible to put 'PIG' into a mileometer:

or any other three-letter word for that matter:

Of course, it isn't enough to code just *letters*. The code should include, say, everything that could be typed on a typewriter (including comma, full stop and of course a space). In order to store something longer than three characters (for instance a name and address) there would have to be several mileometers end to end.

comma 26   *full stop* 27   *space* 28

◀ 181508 041828 031428 190708 182818 141719 281405 281907 081306 27▶

In just the same way letters and other characters can be represented in a binary mileometer (*i.e.* in a computer). Each character must be coded in terms of 0's and 1's using a certain number of bits. For example, it could be done like this:

A	01000001	E	01000101	I	*etc.*
B	01000010	F	01000110		
C	01000011	G	01000111		
D	01000100	H	01001000		

Although not every computer would use the same patterns of bits shown here the idea still applies.

Notice there are three different conventions in this chapter for coding different types of information. If you were to find a string of bits lying in the street you wouldn't know what the string meant unless you knew the convention that had been used to code it.

If you came across a decimal mileometer with 031406 in it what would you conclude? It may be an integer (31,406), or a real number (0.1406×10^{-47}), or a word (DOG). Unless you knew which coding convention had been used you could not know the meaning of 031406.

There is very little information that cannot be represented as numbers or words. If a computer can hold in its memory integer numbers, real numbers and characters then they should be able to cope with almost all types of information stored in offices, factories, universities. What computers can *do* with that information is described in later chapters.

There is inside computers one other kind of information coded in binary. This is in some ways the most important of all. The instructions which make up the program — *telling the computer how to process all the other kinds of information —* are themselves coded as strings of 0's and 1's just like the rest. These instructions are described in the next chapter.

4 HOW DO THEY WORK?
((MACHINE INSTRUCTIONS))

The great power and flexibility of the computer lies in the fact that the instructions it obeys are stored in its memory along with the data to be processed. To understand how this can be it is necessary to know something about the main parts of a computer.

A computer may be thought of as two boxes; the main store or memory (where much of the information is stored), and the central processing unit or CPU (where the information is processed). There are also numerous pieces of machinery (dealt with in Chapter 7) which may be plugged into these boxes.

Inside the main store are masses of binary digits — the 0's and 1's described in the previous chapter. They

⊲ CPU
⊲ MAIN STORE

are not all in a heap however. The main store has lots of little boxes (or shelves or pigeon holes) each with its own row of bits. These boxes are the 'binary mileometers' described in the previous chapter and are called *words*. Within one computer every word has the same number of bits called the *word length*. The word length may be as small as 8 bits, or as big as 60 bits or more, depending on the make of computer.

58	0110100010111
59	0110100111011
60	1001001000101
61	1111101111010
62	0110100110100

⊲ ADDRESSES

The number of words in main store is the memory size of the computer. This may be anything from a few thousand words on the smallest computers to several million on the largest.

Each word (or box) has an address which may be thought of as a number painted on the end of each box. It is by means of this address that information can be put into a particular word and found again when needed.

Information may be moved around inside the computer. If information is sent (in the form of 0's and 1's) to a particular address, what was at that address beforehand is blotted out and overwritten. If information is taken from a certain address, it is simply a *copy* that is taken; the 0's and 1's at that address remain the same.

Inside the CPU is at least one box able to hold the same information as a word of main store. However in the CPU such a box is usually called a _register_ rather than a word. There may be several such registers but hardly ever more than a couple of dozen.

The important thing about the CPU is that information may be *processed* within it. Information may be moved around in the main store, or between main store and CPU, but if it is necessary to do arithmetic on the information it usually has to be done in the CPU.

Describing how computers operate is difficult if the description is in terms of long strings of binary digits. Words of main store and registers in the CPU are very much like binary mileometers, so the computer is described here as if all its words and registers were indeed mileometers — but decimal ones. What has been said about decimal mileometers can, as has been shown, be transferred easily to binary ones.

58	020009
59	150306
60	091406

Take a simple problem to see how it would be performed by computer. Two numbers are to be fed into the computer, added, and the result printed. Two pieces of machinery have to be plugged in to the computer; one for feeding numbers into the computer; another for printing numbers generated by the computer. More is said about such machinery in Chapter 7. At the moment it is assumed there is a typewriter keyboard for feeding numbers in, and some sort of printer for getting numbers out.

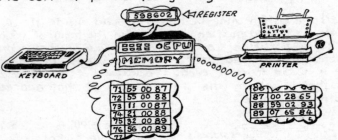

Before the process starts the situation may be as shown in the picture above. A register is shown in the CPU and several words in the main store. The values shown in these mileometers need some explanation. The register and words 87-89 contain values left over from some previous computation. These values are not relevant to the current problem. Words 71-76, on the other hand, contain instructions needed to read two numbers from the keyboard, add them and print the result. (Never mind how these instructions found their way into these locations; that is explained in later chapters.)

No one could know (without being told) that words 71-76 contain the program — the set of instructions. These values could have been data numbers. However, a different convention has been used for coding the new information. Each instruction for this computer has two parts; the *operation code* (the first two digits) and the address of a word of main store (the last four digits).

ADDRESS OF THIS INSTRUCTION → 71 | 55 0087 ← OPERATION CODE
↖ ADDRESS OF A WORD

The operation code indicates what type of action is needed. In our imaginary computer 55 means 'take a number from the keyboard and store it in main store'. The address shows which word of main store is to be used in the operation: word 87.

Each of the instructions from 71 to 76 will be obeyed in turn by the computer. The effect of each instruction is now explained.

[71] [55 0087] A number is taken from the keyboard and placed in word 87 of main store. If the number 15 were typed on the keyboard the result of obeying this instruction would be a change to the value stored at location 87 as shown here. (Because the words are *decimal* mileometers no change to the data is needed. In a real computer the number would have to be changed from decimal to binary.)

[87] [00~~~65~~]
[87] [000015]

[72] [55 0088] The operation code (55) is the same as for the previous operation. Once again a number is taken from the keyboard and placed in a word of main store. This time the word changed is 88 because this is the address given in the instruction. If the number 127 were typed on the keyboard this value would replace the previous contents of word 88.

[88] [000127]

[73] [11 0087] The operation code 11 means 'take a number from a word of main store and copy it into the register'. The address contained within the instruction indicates which word is to be used: word 87. The value in word 87 is then copied into the register. The content of word 87 remains unchanged but the register now has the value shown.

[000015]
REGISTER

[74] [21 0088] The operation code 21 means 'take a number from a word of main store and *add* it into the register'. Remember that the CPU is the place where arithmetic is usually done. The word to be used is 88. The value in word 88 (*ie.* 127) is

added to the value in the register (*i.e.* 15), the result (*i.e.* 142) being left in the register. The value in word 88 remains unchanged.

[75] [320089] The operation code 32 means 'take a number from the register and copy it into a word of main store'. The destination of the value is to be word 89. This instruction causes the previous number in word 89 to be overwritten with the value from the register (*i.e.* 142). The contents of the register remain unchanged (*i.e.* 142).

[76] [560089] The operation code 56 means 'take a number from a word of main store and send it to the printer'. The rest of the instruction indicates that word 89 is the one to be used. This instruction causes the value in word 89 (*i.e.* 142) to be printed on paper by the printer. The content of word 89 remains unchanged. (In a real computer the value would have to be converted from binary to decimal. But because this imaginary computer works in decimal the conversion is *not* needed.)

That may seem a *very* cumbersome way to add two numbers. Although computer instructions are obeyed rapidly (about a million per second) each instruction does very little. The operation codes shown here are particular to our imaginary computer (using mileometers) but *the* kinds of operation performed closely match those carried out by real computer instructions.

71	550087
72	550088
73	110087
74	210088
75	320089
76	560089

On page 20 it had to be explained that the instructions comprising the program were in words 71 to 76 on the diagram. How does the computer know that this is where the instructions are? The program is not necessarily in the same place every time the computer is used. It would

be disastrous if, for instance, the computer were to obey
the data in words 87 to 89 *as if they were instructions.*

The answer is that the CPU has a special register
called the *sequence register*. This register always holds
the address of the next instruction to be obeyed. When
the computer needs to know what to do next it always
refers to this register. When the computer has taken
note of the address stored in this register — and is
about to obey the instruction stored at that address —
the sequence register clicks on so that it now contains
the address of the next instruction, and so on. The
value 71 must first be placed in the sequence register
if instructions starting in word 71 are to be obeyed.

ARITHMETIC REGISTER   SEQUENCE REGISTER

One might ask what would happen when the instruction in word 76 had been obeyed. Because the
computer obeys instructions in sequence the register
clicks on to 77. When the computer has finished obeying the instruction in word 76 the sequence register shows
that the next instruction is to be found in word 77.
But is there an instruction there to be obeyed? If so
what about word word 78? It would appear that
before long the computer would be trying to obey the
instruction in word 87; but word 87
does not contain an instruction at all.
This problem may be avoided by
placing a special instruction in word 77.

`77` `430071`

Now as soon as the instruction in word 76 has
been obeyed the computer finds address 77 in the
sequence register. The computer then takes the instruction in word 77 as the next instruction to be obeyed. At
that moment the sequence register clicks on automatically to 78. So far nothing new has happened. But
then the computer starts to obey the instruction 430071.
Operation code 43 means 'take the address in this
instruction and copy it into the sequence register'. The
address in this instruction is 0071 `000142`
so this replaces the previous contents `78` `0071`
of the sequence register. `CPU`

*N*ow when the computer consults the sequence register it finds the next instruction to be obeyed is in word 71. This causes the process to start all over again, reading two more numbers from the keyboard, adding them, and printing the new result. Once again when word 77 is reached control would be transferred to the instruction in word 71. The instructions from word 71 to word 77 would be obeyed over and over until the computer is switched off — or until something equally drastic happens. A set of instructions which is to be obeyed repeatedly is called, in computer terms, a *loop*.

*L*oops are very important in computer programming. Work for a computer is often repetitive and can be performed by means of instructions in a loop. For example, instead of reading numbers to be added together, the loop could cause the current and previous settings of a gas meter to be read; the cost calculated; the account printed. Then the computer would do the same thing with data for another gas meter, and so on.

*T*he computer instruction being obeyed at any time *controls* the computer. An instruction (like that at word 77) which gives control to an instruction somewhere else is called a *transfer of control* instruction. Whenever word 77 is obeyed control is passed elsewhere, so this is called an *unconditional* transfer of control. A computer also has *conditional* transfer of control instructions. For instance, control may be transferred if a certain number is bigger than zero. If it is not bigger then the instruction following in the usual sequence is next obeyed.

*E*ach computer instruction does only a small amount of work. This is to keep the electronics comparatively simple. Each instruction has to be carried out by means of electrical circuits. An example to show how this can be done is presented in the next chapter.

5 HOW DO THEY DO IT?
(HARDWARE OPERATIONS)

The last chapter spoke about *obeying* instructions. How can electronic circuitry *obey* a set of 0's and 1's ? To answer that question it is necessary to understand how 0's and 1's are moved around within the computer.

Every computer has within it a _clock_ which generates electrical pulses at a constant rate; usually several million per second.

The clock pulses are used to carry bits around within the computer. Suppose for example the bits stored in a certain word are to be moved into a register. The bits in the word may be stored as cores of mag- netic material (see page 12) or as tiny circuits, some conducting and some not. Wires carry a clock pulse into each of the bits of the word. The electronics ensure that 0 bits prevent the pulse travelling on where- as 1 bits allow the pulse to pass through.

Output wires carry bits coded as pulses. (A pulse travelling along a wire represents a 1. If there is no pulse on a wire when a clock pulse is due that wire is said to be carrying a 0. The pulses can now be carried to the register along the wires, and can be used to change the values of bits stored in the register.

For ease of description in the previous chapter computer instructions were described as though they were decimal numbers. In real computers they are binary numbers, some of the bits being the operation code and some representing the address. (Addresses of words are also represented in binary.)

ADDRESS OF THIS INSTRUCTION   OPERATION CODE   ADDRESS OF A WORD

Computer circuits contain many switches so that electrical pulses may be routed along different paths depending on switch settings. The switches may be

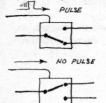

PULSE

NO PULSE

turned on or off rapidly (within a few thousandths of a millionth of a second). Switching may be performed by means of an electrical pulse. When a pulse is received the switch is turned one way; when no pulse is received the other.

In early computers switching was done by means of relays. The pulse was sent through an electro magnet which pulled a piece of metal from one contact to another. Now it is all done by electronics so there are no moving parts to slow things down. Electronic switching can be performed in a few *nanoseconds*. (A thousand nanoseconds make a *micro-second* ; a million microseconds make a second.)

Now it is possible to show how a binary instruction such as the one above may be used to move information out of a particular word. The address portion of the instruction causes switches to be set so that the clock pulse is sent to the correct word. (An address of only four bits is used here so as to simplify the diagram opposite.)

The clock pulse is sent to all the bits in word 0110 so that these bits are carried along wires to be used as needed.

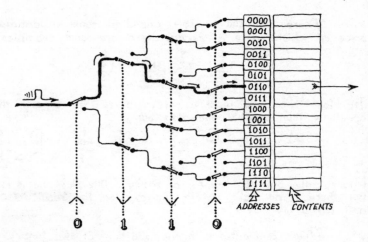

ADDRESSES   CONTENTS

0 1 1 0

The bits of the operation code also cause switches to be set so that the data bits are routed through those parts of the CPU that perform appropriate operations on them. For example if the operation code means 'add the contents of a word to the contents of a register and store the result in the register' then the following circuit is set up.

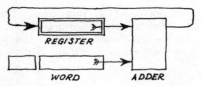

REGISTER

WORD   ADDER

Although this diagram shows connexions as single lines there would in each case be enough wires to carry *all* bits from the word and register.

Inside the box labelled 'Adder' two binary numbers are added; the result appears on the wires leading out of the box. How can it be done? To answer this question it is necessary first to understand what adding binary numbers entails.

There are 100 possible one-digit sums in decimal, some of which cause a *carry*. Here are some examples:

$$\frac{4}{\underset{4}{+0}} \qquad \frac{2}{\underset{7}{+5}} \qquad \frac{5}{\underset{7}{+2}} \qquad \frac{3}{\underset{12}{+9}} \qquad \frac{8}{\underset{15}{+7}}$$

The last two sums have a carry of 1. In binary there are only four possible one-digit sums:

A $\quad \frac{0}{\underset{0}{+0}} \qquad$ **B** $\quad \frac{0}{\underset{1}{+1}} \qquad$ **C** $\quad \frac{1}{\underset{1}{+0}} \qquad$ **D** $\quad \frac{1}{\underset{10}{+1}}$

where only sum D causes a carry. One plus one is two but there is no digit '2' in binary, so the result is 0 and *carry* 1.

When confronted with the addition of two binary numbers it may be easier for human beings to translate them into decimal, do a decimal addition and then translate the result back into binary.

$$
\begin{array}{llllllllll}
0111 & \Rightarrow & 0\times8 & + & 1\times4 & + & 1\times2 & + & 1\times1 & = & 7 \\
+\,0101 & \Rightarrow & 0\times8 & + & 1\times4 & + & 0\times2 & + & 1\times1 & = & 5 \\
\hline
1100 & \Leftarrow & 1\times8 & + & 1\times4 & + & 0\times2 & + & 0\times1 & = & 12
\end{array}
$$

Computers do not work in this way. They carry out a binary addition. This proceeds just as when adding decimal numbers, starting at the right-hand end, adding a digit from each number at a time, carrying digits where necessary.

$$
\begin{array}{l}
0\ 1\ 1\ 1 \\
+\ 0\ 1\ 0\ 1 \\
\underline{\quad 1\ 1 \quad} \\
1\ 1\ 0\ 0
\end{array}
$$

The tiny 1's are those that have been carried. Apart from the digits in the right-hand column, addition at every position may involve *three* bits, two of them being digits from the original numbers (which will be called the data bits) and the third the carry digit from the next position to the right (which will be called the carry-in). An example is shown in the dotted box above.

A mechanism for adding two binary digits is called in computer jargon a *half adder.* This is because it takes two of them to cope with the three bits at each position in a sum. A half adder takes as its input two binary digits and produces a result digit and a carry digit (which may be 0 if there is no carry). The four possible situations for a half adder exactly parallel the four one-digit sums A to D shown opposite:

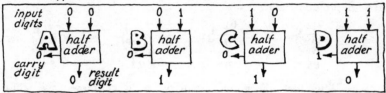

Adding in the carry digit from the next position to the right requires another half adder.

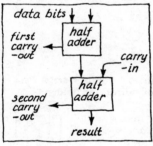

At first sight it may appear that we need yet another half adder to combine the two carry-outs — and so produce a single carry-in — for the next position to the left. The first carry-out is zero except when the data bits are both 1 (as in case D above). In that case the result from the first half-adder is 0. So the bottom half adder can only produce a second carry-out of 0.

In fact it is impossible for both carry-outs to be 1. Either both of them are 0 (in which case 0 should be carried) or one of them is 1 (in which case 1 should be carried).

It is easy to build a piece of circuitry having two input wires and one output wire — and which sends a pulse on the output wire (if it receives a pulse on either (or both) input wires) This is the device needed to combine the two carry-outs. It emits a pulse if it receives one at the first input wire OR at the second, so it is called an OR-gate and is represented by a special symbol. Four diagrams of an OR-gate under all possible conditions are shown below.

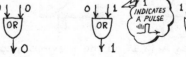

Another piece of circuitry is similar, but only (sends on a pulse if it receives pulses simultaneously on the first input wire AND the second input wire.) This is called an <u>AND-gate</u>. Its four possible conditions are depicted below:

The last piece of circuitry is a perverse one which (does NOT send on a pulse if it receives one, but does send on a pulse if it has NOT received one) This is called a <u>NOT-gate</u>. It has only two possible conditions as depicted below:

Now we have enough electronic components to make a half adder. It has the following structure:

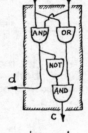

The input bits come from points *a* and *b*. Connexions of the wires are such that the input bits arrive both at the AND-gate and at the OR-gate at the top of the half adder. Because there are only four possibilities for the two input bits there are only four possible conditions for the half adder. These possible conditions are depicted below. Compare inputs and outputs

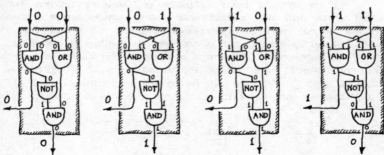

with those on sketches A to D on the previous page.

By using several half adders and OR-gates one full
adder may be constructed. This copes with binary numbers
more than one digit long.

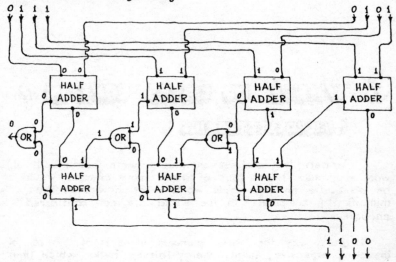

By extending this circuit to the left, binary integers
of any length may be added automatically. The diagram
above shows the addition of the two four-digit numbers
used as an example on page 28. But the circuit will
add *any* two four-digit numbers. Within one clock pulse
the result appears on the output wires.

Addition is possible by electronic means; so are
other arithmetic operations. Negative numbers are usually
stored in such a way that subtraction can be performed
by making a number negative and adding it. Multiplic-
ation may be done by repeated additions; division by
repeated subtractions. But there are much faster methods
than these. The methods are also inherently simple
because the information on which they operate is coded
in binary.

It should be clear from this small example that
computer circuits are complicated and require many components. The next chapter describes some ways in which
such circuits are mass produced.

6 WHERE DO CHIPS COME IN ?
(MICROELECTRONICS)

When the earliest computers were being built it was supposed that four of them, more or less, would be adequate for the whole world. Yet now even the millions of computers in the world are not considered enough.

In a way the early pioneers were right. A few of the slow, expensive, huge, energy-thirsty hulks which then existed would have been quite enough. But computers are no longer like that. A revolution has taken place in the way computers are made. This is due to things called _silicon chips_. What are these chips and how do they affect computers ?

The short answer is that (silicon chips enable complicated electronic circuits to be produced which are tiny, run on very little power, and cost next to nothing.) The longer answer involves a survey of electronics during this century.

It is well known that metals, especially copper and silver, are good conductors of electricity. Some materials are very bad conductors (or good insulators), notably paper, glass, wax and ceramics. (The good conductors have many electrons which are free to wander through the material.) Because electrons are negatively charged, if all these free electrons wander in one direction the substance carries an electric current. In bad conductors almost all the electrons are closely tied to the atoms so they cannot move.

Other materials are neither very good nor very bad conductors. These are called *semiconductors*. Apart from their conductivity, semiconductors can display electrical peculiarities.

Crystals of certain semiconductor materials allow electricity to pass in one direction but not in the other. This is the basis of the 'crystal set' radio which detects radio waves but does not amplify them. So the sound they produce is usually faint.

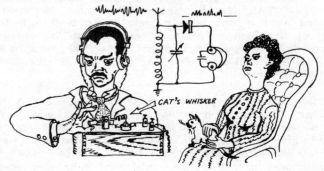

CAT'S WHISKER

Pure crystals would not show this effect but would be bad conductors — because they would have no free electrons. Some impurities cause an area of the crystal to have an excess of free electrons; others create an area that can receive free electrons. Electrons can flow from the first kind of area to the second kind, but not in the reverse direction.

When radio broadcasting started crystal sets were popular. The right kind of area on the crystal had to be found by prodding the crystal with a fine wire called a 'cat's whisker'. This operation was called 'tickling in'. Crystal sets were soon displaced by radio receivers using vacuum tubes. A vacuum tube is a glass tube with the air pumped out and containing several metal plates. One plate has to be heated by a filament until it releases electrons into the vacuum. A current can then flow across from one plate to another; electrical impulses on a grid of wires between the two plates can thereby be amplified. The volume of sound may then be as loud as you like.

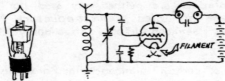

The first computers also used vacuum tubes — thousands of them. Their power requirements were huge, and so was their heat output because most of the power was consumed by heater filaments. Someone predicted that if a computer were to be built with the power of the human brain it would need the energy of Niagara falls to power it and the waters of Niagara to cool it. And it would probably take the Empire State building to house it.

No one had any intention of building such a large computer, however. It would not have worked for more than a few seconds at a time. Vacuum tubes had a limited life because their filaments burned out (just like those of domestic light bulbs). When a tube 'blew' the computer was out of action until that tube was replaced. The more tubes there were, the more often one blew.

Then it was discovered that semiconductors could be used to amplify electrical signals. Materials such as germanium and silicon were employed. Controlled amounts of impurities of different kinds had to be introduced. Then (a 'sandwich' of semiconductors with different impurities was made. Electrical impulses on one of the pieces would produce amplified electric currents between the other two) The *transistor* was born.

SILICON WITH
ONE IMPURITY

SILICON WITH
ANOTHER

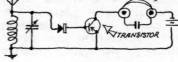

🅐 new set of computers soon emerged — the so-called 'second generation' computers. Where the older machines used tubes for gates and switches, the new machines used transistors. The advantages of transistors over vacuum tubes were that they were smaller, more reliable and needed less power. They did not need a heating element. More powerful computers could be made which would still fit into a large room. Main store was usually made of magnetic cores — little rings of magnetic material as illustrated on page 12. In order to conserve space the cores were made as small as possible. Three wires had to be threaded through the hole in the middle of the ring.

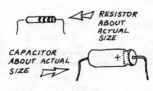

TRANSISTOR ABOUT ACTUAL SIZE

CORE, ABOUT ACTUAL SIZE ⇨ ·

RESISTOR ABOUT ACTUAL SIZE

CAPACITOR ABOUT ACTUAL SIZE ⇨

⊙f course, these are not the only components used in computers. Res-istors (which electric current has difficulty in passing through) and capacitors (which can store electric charge) were also used in the cir-cuitry of the AND-, OR- and NOT-gates.

🆃he components described above varied in size according to capacity and power requirement, but typical sizes are shown.

🅸n order (to cut down the cost of wiring up the thou-sands of components needed for a computer) (and in order to improve reliability) printed circuits were used. These are also used in domestic electronic equipment; you can see one by looking inside any modern radio or tele-vision receiver. (A printed circuit board is a thin sheet of insulating material dotted with holes.) On one side the components are placed with their wires sticking through the holes. On the other side a design has been 'etched' in copper and covered with molten solder. (The process of etching is described overleaf.) The pattern forms all the

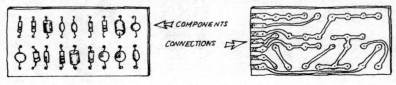

⟵ COMPONENTS

CONNECTIONS ⇨

connections between components. Often at the edge of a board are gold-plated copper strips which fit into a socket through which wires lead to other printed circuit boards.

Printed circuits proved a great boon. The quest for smaller and better circuits has not stopped, however. How can circuits be made which take less space to store, less power to run, less money to manufacture? Printing the the wiring on a board helps a great deal. But making the wiring any smaller is not much help while the components (resistors, capacitors, transistors) remain the same size. The breakthrough was the realization that the components themselves could be built up by printing successive layers on the board. Now the components are so tiny they cannot be seen without a microscope.

(The material used as the base plate is silicon.) This is one of the commonest elements on earth. Silicon dioxide is the main constituent of sand. <u>Pure silicon is an insulator</u>, and the silicon used as 'base plates' must be 99.9999999 % pure. Measured amounts of an impurity are then added to make it a semiconductor. Wafer-thin sheets of such silicon 10 cm across and 0.5 mm thick are polished to give a very flat, smooth surface. The flat sheets then undergo a number of processes which deposit transistors, resistors, capacitors and 'connecting wires' on the surface.

The processes used to do this are similar to those used for etching. — a form of art more popular in previous centuries than today. A copper plate was thinly coated with wax, then a design traced using a stylus with a sharp point which scratched through the wax. The plate was then moistened with acid which bit only into the parts where the wax coating had been scratched away. When the acid and remaing wax had been removed the design remained 'etched' into the metal plate which was then used as a printing plate to make one or more 'etchings' on paper.

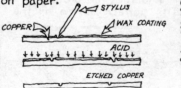

STYLUS

COPPER

WAX COATING

ACID

ETCHED COPPER

ETCHING

The wafers of silicon are coated, not with wax, but with a material called 'photoresist'. This is a kind of (plastic which can be hardened by exposure to ultra-violet light.) The wafers are covered with a mask — like a photographic negative — before being exposed to ultra-violet light, when parts of the photoresist become hardened but not others. Washing with a solvent removes only the soft photoresist, leaving areas of silicon exposed for further treatments.

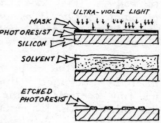

Various types of treatment are possible. The wafers may be heated in gases which cause layers of substances to be deposited on the exposed surface. Silicon layers with different impurities can build up tiny transistors. Silicon dioxide can be deposited where an insulator is needed. Aluminium can be evaporated on to the surface to form 'connecting wires' of conducting material — doing the job previously done by the printed circuit board.

After each treatment the remaining photoresist is removed with a solvent. Then a new film of photoresist is applied, a new mask is used, a new treatment applied, and so on, until the silicon plate is covered with a three-dimensional mosaic of patches of material. The electrical components required are built on the surface, and so this is called an *integrated circuit*. (IC)

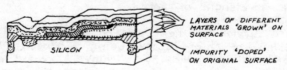

LAYERS OF DIFFERENT MATERIALS 'GROWN' ON SURFACE

IMPURITY 'DOPED' ON ORIGINAL SURFACE

The masks for each treatment may be produced photographically. Because of this it is possible to reduce them in size enormously. In fact the masks for one 10 cm wide wafer of silicon may contain several hundred copies of the same pattern, so that when all the processes have been applied the wafer is cut up into *chips* — each perhaps 0.5 cm square — all of them identical.

Just before the wafers are cut into chips they are tested by a computer-controlled machine that places tiny probes on each chip in turn to test whether it functions correctly. If it does not, the chip is dabbed with a spot of paint to flag it as useless. A yield of 40 functioning chips from a wafer containing several hundred is considered adequate return.

When the chips have been separated the good ones must be packaged. This involves attaching gold wires to the tiny contacts on the edges of the chip and attaching the other ends to stout pins for connection to a circuit board. A plastic cover is then moulded over the chip, leaving the pins sticking out like legs.

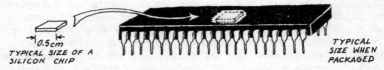

←0.5cm→
TYPICAL SIZE OF A
SILICON CHIP

TYPICAL
SIZE WHEN
PACKAGED

Transistors used to be the most expensive components in computer circuitry — on chips they are the easiest components to build and therefore the cheapest. The capacity of a chip is usually expressed in terms of the number of components (such as transistors, resistors, capacitors) that it contains. It is now possible to have hundreds of thousands of components on one chip. There is a limit to the reduction of size possible using photographic masks — the current limiting factor being the wavelength of light.

What can the circuit on a chip do? An enormous variety of chips is now being produced. (A digital watch is controlled by a chip) A pocket calculator has a chip which contains a hundred times as many transistors as a radio or television receiver.

Large computers now have many printed circuit boards covered, not with traditional components, but with chips. It is possible to produce a complete CPU for a small computer on one chip — a *microprocessor*. It is also possible for one chip to contain large amounts of main store. Although cores can be made very small they are *enormous* compared with the components of an integrated circuit. By means of representing each bit as a switching circuit, (65,000 bits can be stored on one chip.) Chips may also serve as adaptors between a computer and devices for reading and writing information as described in the next chapter. Some chips have been produced which have CPU, store and input/output adaptors — a complete *microcomputer* — all on the one chip.

A chip takes up very little space. Its power requirements are tiny. It is highly reliable. How much does one cost? Although the equipment for making silicon wafers and the photographic masks is high, although designing a chip is very expensive and although most of them are thrown away at the testing stage, because chips can be mass-produced each one may cost as little as a ham sandwich or, for complicated chips, as much as a good meal in a restaurant.

The picture below shows one of the many photographic masks needed to produce a chip. This one is the Ferranti ULA final interconnection mask used in the manufacture of the ULA range of semi-custom integrated circuits.

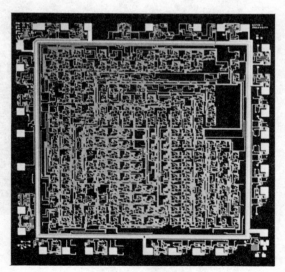

Ferranti Limited

The picture below shows the Ferranti F100-L microprocessor chip. Gold wires connecting the chip to pins in the surrounding package can be seen. The actual size of the chip is half a centimetre square. On the opposite page is a more detailed view of the surface of the chip.

Ferranti Limited

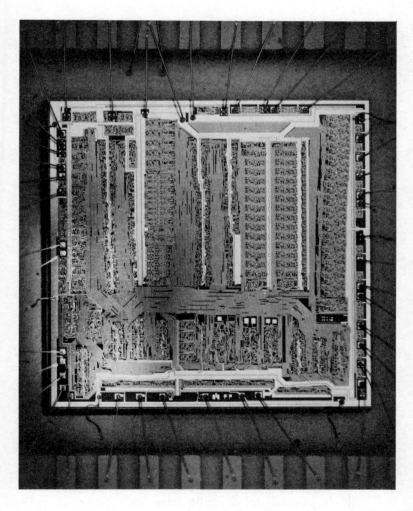

Ferranti Limited

7 WHAT CAN YOU PLUG IN ?
(PERIPHERAL DEVICES)

Though the computer can carry out its operations rapidly, this is not much help if you can't get data into it. And when the computer has finished work the results are no use unless seen. _Peripheral devices_ (peripherals for short) plug into the computer and serve as its ears, eyes, hands and voice — providing two-way communication between the computer and the outside world.

Electric drills may vary in appearance but the variety of accessories that can be attached is far greater. Similarly computers differ in shape and size but the diversity among peripherals is far greater. This is not surprising considering the great range of things they have to do.

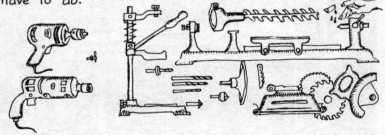

It is possible to describe here only some of the more common computer peripherals.

One of the traditional ways of getting information into a computer is by means of punched cards.

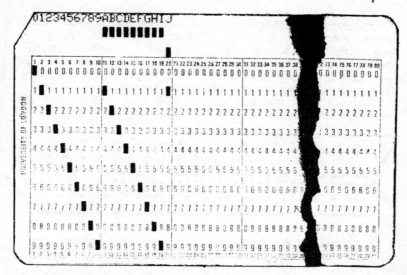

Punched cards are made accurately the same size and shape. Holes are punched into the card to represent letters and other characters. Up to 80 characters can be coded on one card, each character represented by (a pattern of holes in a narrow vertical slice) called a _column_. At the top of each column the character is printed for quick recognition by eye. Cards are punched and printed in a desk-shaped machine called a *keypunch*. After they have been punched and checked the cards may be fed into a _card reader_. The card reader is a peripheral which passes cards one by one under wire brushes. When a hole passes beneath a brush, its wires make contact with a plate at the other side of the card, thus sensing the presence of a hole.

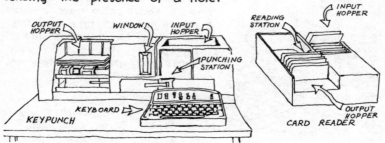

KEYPUNCH — OUTPUT HOPPER, WINDOW, INPUT HOPPER, PUNCHING STATION, KEYBOARD

CARD READER — READING STATION, INPUT HOPPER, OUTPUT HOPPER

Punched paper tape, like punched cards, has characters coded as patterns of holes. However, paper tape comes as a continuous long strip, perhaps many metres in length. The smaller holes are there to guide the tape through the reader. The larger holes represent data, each stripe across the tape representing one character. The characters are coded in binary form, a hole representing a 1 and no hole representing a 0.

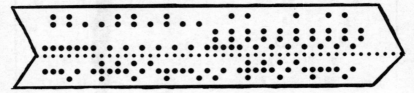

Paper tape is punched on a machine looking like a typewriter. This is called a *teletypewriter* (or *teletype* for short). Every time a key is pressed, not only is the letter typed on a sheet of paper; the code for that character is also punched onto a length of paper tape which gradually emerges from the device. When the tape is ready it may be fed into a computer by means of a *paper tape reader*. This passes the paper tape between a light and a row of photo-electric cells. When a hole comes along the light shines through and causes a pulse of electricity to flow from the photo-electric cell.

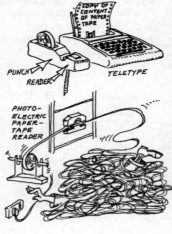

PUNCH
READER TELETYPE

PHOTO-
ELECTRIC
PAPER-
TAPE
READER

Unlike punched cards, paper tape does not have characters typed on it, so it is harder to find out what characters have been coded just by looking at the tape. But teletypes which have a punch also have a reader. If you fit a paper tape into this it will drive the teletype like a player piano – typing on a sheet of paper just what characters are punched into the tape.

It is possible for output from a computer to be transmitted via paper tape. Some computers have a *paper tape punch* as a peripheral. The information punched by the computer on this tape may then be 'played' on a teletype so as to produce a readable copy. However, there are faster ways of obtaining readable output.

Large computers produce most printed output on a device called a _lineprinter_. Unlike a typewriter (which types one character at a time) (a lineprinter prints all the characters for one line at the same time)— hence its name. Sheets of paper joined to one another and perforated at the edges are pulled through the device. There are several different designs for lineprinters. In one common type a rapidly spinning drum has all the characters embossed on it at every print position across the sheet. When the right character comes opposite the paper, a hammer knocks the paper against the inked ribbon so that the letter is printed on the paper.

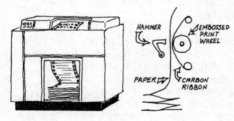

Accounts for gas, electricity, telephone _etc._ are printed on lineprinters. Some lineprinters are able to print several thousand lines a minute and are expensive.

Earlier it was said that a teletype may be used to prepare paper tape for input to a computer or to type the contents of a paper tape which a computer has punched. We may dispense with the paper tape altogether and simply use the teletype as a combined input and output device.

When you type on such a teletype the characters appear on the sheet of paper just as with a normal typewriter, but electrical signals simultaneosly transmit characters to the computer. When the computer sends information to the teletype this information appears as characters typed on the sheet of paper. When a teletype is used as a computer peripheral in such a way it is called a _terminal_ (or a _keyboard terminal_ to be more precise ; other peripherals can also be called terminals).

Another kind of keyboard terminal is a _visual display unit_ or _VDU_. Like a teletype it has a typewriter keyboard but instead of typing on paper it displays characters on a sort of television screen. The record is not permanent, but a screenful of information can be seen at any one time.

It is often necessary to store large amounts of information for long periods; for example the names and addresses of all electricity customers. Cards and paper tape are bulky, heavy and slow to read into a computer. Though some card readers read several hundred cards a minute — some paper tape readers read 1,000 characters a second — these are slow peripherals for a computer.

(Magnetic tapes are used to hold large quantities of information). The tape itself is similar to that used for ordinary reel-to-reel tape recorders except it is wider. The surface of the tape is covered with iron oxide which is magnetic. The information is coded as tiny patches magnetized in one direction or the other. A magnetic tape the size of a dinner plate may contain as much information as a roomful of punched cards, and is quicker to read. (The computer peripheral used to read and write magnetic tapes is called a _tape drive_)

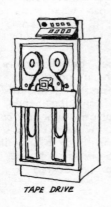

TAPE DRIVE

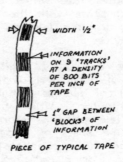

WIDTH ½"

INFORMATION ON 9 'TRACKS' AT A DENSITY OF 800 BITS PER INCH OF TAPE

1" GAP BETWEEN 'BLOCKS' OF INFORMATION

PIECE OF TYPICAL TAPE

TYPICAL REEL OF TAPE ABOUT THE SIZE OF A DINNER PLATE

Also used for storing large amounts of information are *magnetic disks*. Disks are like long playing records but coated with a magnetic oxide. Sometimes several plates are fastened together by a central spindle. They are used on a peripheral known as a *disk drive* on which they are rapidly spun.

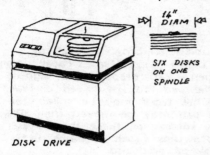

14" DIAM

SIX DISKS
ON ONE
SPINDLE

DISK DRIVE

If magnetic tape is similar to the reels used with a domestic tape recorder then magnetic disks are similar to records. In order to listen to a track near the far end of a tape it is necessary to wind all the way up to it. With a record, on the other hand, it is possible to select any track immediately. The same factors apply to computer tapes and disks.

Disks and disk drives are expensive. They are used only on large computers for situations where the information is needed quickly and the order in which it will be required is not known in advance.

An example of this is given by bank accounts. In the branches of a bank there may be VDU's which are connected to a central computer. In order to find out details of a customer's account the bank clerk types a question on a VDU. The computer needs to select details for that account rapidly because the clerk is waiting for an answer. In order to do this, accounts are usually stored on disks rather than magnetic tapes at the central computer.

For small computers a much cheaper kind of disk is available. This is like a singles record inside a cardboard sleeve. It is flexible, hence the name *floppy disk*. The corresponding peripheral (called a *floppy disk drive*) has a slot into which the disk is pushed — still in its sleeve. The disk is spun and the information read through a window cut in the sleeve. A floppy disk cannot hold as much information as a

'hard' disk; nor can information be retrieved so rapidly.
Floppy disks are particularly useful with microcomputers
(see Chapter 12).

READING
WINDOW
CUT IN
SLEEVE

8" FLOPPY DISK

FLEXIBLE

FLOPPY DISK
DRIVES

SLOT

A computer is enabled to draw pictures by
means of a peripheral called _a plotter_. Paper from
a roll moves under a pen. In response to signals
sent from the computer the pen may be raised or lower-
ed (to touch the paper); the paper may be rolled for-
wards or backwards; the pen may be moved from side
to side on a gantry. By means of these three types
of movement accurate drawings (such as maps and
engineering drawings) may be produced.

A plotter is a fairly expensive instrument but
cheaper ones are coming on the market as plotters
become more popular. Some VDU's are capable of
displaying pictures (in colour) as well as characters. They
are then called _graphics terminals_.

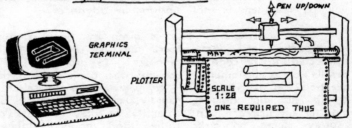

GRAPHICS
TERMINAL

PLOTTER

PEN UP/DOWN

MAP

SCALE
1:28
ONE REQUIRED THUS

Many, many other peripherals are capable of
being plugged into a computer. There are optical
character recognition (OCR) readers that can read
typewritten letters; printers that can produce at high
speed half-tone pictures as well as characters; even
peripherals that recognise (limited) spoken words or
produce output in _spoken form_.

CAESAR SHOULD INITIATE PREVENTIVE
SECURITY MEASURES ON MARCH 15

It is sometimes possible to connect a peripheral to a computer by means of a telephone line. This means, for instance, that someone who owns a terminal may telephone a computer bureau and use the bureau computer — paying according to the amount of use.

TO THE COMPUTER BUREAU

It is also possible for two computers to be connected to one another (by direct link or via telephone line). Each computer may treat the other one as if it were a peripheral such as a terminal. Information may be sent directly from one computer to another. This is the way that computer networks are established, each computer performing its own work and also forwarding to other computers in the network the data they need.

8 WHAT DO THEY UNDERSTAND?

(PROGRAMMING LANGUAGES)

In the last few chapters the emphasis has been increasingly on (the physical bits and pieces that make up a computer — the *hardware*). The hardware of a computer is controlled by (sets of instructions or programs — the *software*.) Computers would not be nearly so useful if programs could not be written to make them do different things. This chapter faces the problem of how to communicate a program to a computer.

The program for a computer is like a musical score for an orchestra, a knitting pattern for a knitter, a recipe for a chef. If the instructions are clearly written and followed carefully the desired result is achieved.

So how does one write a program for a computer? A program (of sorts) has already been presented in Chapter 4. That was a program for the 'mileometer' computer. All its instructions were decimal numbers. The only instructions real computers understand are coded in binary form. So, if the computer is to obey the program, the set of instructions ends up looking something like this:

```
0100101100000100
1011011100001010
1101101100000110
0100101100000110
```

and so on, with very much more of it. Such a program is very hard to write, harder to correct and murderous to understand. Nobody should have to do it.

There was a time when people had to write programs in binary. It took a long time and was very difficult, but they managed it. As you might imagine, faced with such a feat of the intellect they soon devised ways of making the task easier.

One of the ways they hit upon was to devise the program not in binary but in some more comprehensible form — then to translate the program into binary when they were happy with it. This is a much easier way to approach the problem. If you had to write an after dinner speech to be delivered in good French you might find it easier to think through the problems whilst writing the speech in English — and only translate it into French when you had got the content right.

How would you write a program if you didn't *have* to write it in binary but could please yourself? Suppose the program was required to read two numbers from the input (say a keyboard), add them together and print the result (say on a printer). You might, for instance, write a program something like this 🡒

A program in such a form is easy to write, easy to understand and easy to correct. But how could it be translated into machine instructions?

```
INPUT X
INPUT Y
LET Z = X + Y
PRINT Z
```

This program does exactly the same things as the mileometer computer program on page 20. So the program in words 71 to 76 on that page gives a translation (into the mileometer computer language) of the program here (in semi-English form). A comparison of corresponding instructions in the two programs shows how translation is performed.

In order to distinguish the two types of notation for a program, the instructions on page 20 will be described as *machine language* , whereas those above will be called *programming language* instructions.

001 00 111 1010 110 THEN 1010
AND YOU CAN'T MISS IT

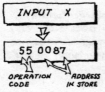

This instruction takes a number typed at the keyboard and places it in a word of main store. INPUT in the programming language instruction corresponds to operation code 55 in the machine instruction. Whereas the machine instruction has to give the address of a word of main store (87), the programming language instruction can refer to this location by means of a more convenient name (X). X simply means 'a word in main store — anywhere will do'.

```
INPUT Y
   ⇩
55 0088
```

Once again INPUT corresponds to operation code 55. The number read from the keyboard must go into a different word of main store from that used for X because a different name is used in the programming language instruction (Y). In the machine instruction address 88 is used.

```
LET Z = X + Y
     ⇩
11 0087
21 0088
32 0089
```

In this case one programming language instruction corresponds to three machine instructions. The value stored in X (word 87) must be copied into the register (operation code 11). The value stored in Y (word 88) must be added into the register (operation code 21). Finally the value in the register must be copied into a word of main store (operation code 32). The word used is referred to as Z in the programming language instruction. In the machine instruction an address different from that of X or Y is needed; 89 will do.

```
PRINT Z
   ⇩
56 0089
```

This instruction corresponds to operation code 56. When specifying the word of main store whose value is to be printed, the programming language instruction can use the name Z. A previous machine instruction has already used word 89 to correspond with Z, so Z must be translated as 89 here also.

This example serves to show the kind of way in which a program — in a notation devised for the convenience of human beings — may be translated into a machine program. However, even with the help of an easy notation like this, translating into binary machine instructions is a thankless task. There must be a better and easier way of programming a computer. And indeed there is.

The hardest part of the process is translating the easy notation into binary instructions.) Computers are supposed to save people from drudgery. How about making the computer do the work? Programs could then be written in the kind of notation that people find most suitable — and the computer would translate them into machine instructions.

So what is needed is a program that will translate programming language instructions into binary machine instructions. This program does, of course, have to be written in binary machine instructions or the computer would not be able to obey it. This may sound like 'Catch 22'. It is possible to save the labour of writing a program in binary provided that you first write a program in binary...

It is not as bad as it sounds, however. Once the program to translate instructions into binary has been written it will translate *all* programs written in the easy notation; it is a binary program to end all binary programs. Once such a translator program is available it should not be necessary to write any more programs as binary machine instructions.

Translation programs like this have been written. They are called _compilers_. (A compiler is a program that takes as its data a program — which a programmer has written — and translates it into binary instructions) the computer can understand. The original program goes through two operations: *compilation* (in which it is translated or *compiled*) and *execution* (in which the compiled program is obeyed).

At compilation time the set of *data* is your *program*; the *output* is once again your program but in a different form. It is not until execution time that your program — newly translated — could be obeyed by the computer; your data read; your results printed.

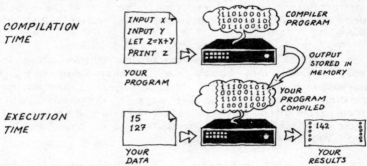

With this scheme of operations the computer is never trying to obey any other kind of instructions than binary ones. Yet we have managed to get the computer to execute a program written in a simple and intelligible notation. The overall effect is as if the computer could *understand* this notation whereas all it really understands is binary.

The notation devised in this chapter to illustrate an easy way of writing programs looks rather like a new language. Writing a compiler is like 'teaching' the computer to understand this language.

How many languages can a computer understand? On the one hand no computer understands any other language than its own familiar 0's and 1's. On the other hand each computer *appears* to understand every language for which a compiler is available on that computer.

The number of programming languages that has been invented (and for which compilers have been written) is enormous. Their names alone would fill a whole chapter if not a book. Fortran (used for much scientific and space programming), Cobol (for business), BASIC, PL/I, APL, Snobol, Pascal, Algol and Ada are some of the more widely known. Each language has its devotees. None of these languages would be of very much interest were it not for the fact that compilers can translate programs written in these languages into a form computers can obey.

```
      WRITE (6,10)
10  FORMAT (1X, 7HTOO BAD)
      STOP
      END
```

```
begin
    for i := 1 step 1 until 50 do
        a[i] := a[i-1]
end
```

```
10  FOR I = 1 TO 2
20  FOR J = 1 TO 3
30  LET A(J,I) = B(I,J)
40  NEXT J
50  NEXT I
```

[2] Z ← 1+(v/,~X ∈ 0 1)+v/,(X<-2*31)v(X≥2*31)vX≠LX

HOW'S THAT AGAIN?

9 HOW DO YOU PROGRAM THEM ?
(PROGRAMMING)

The last chapter showed how computers could be made to understand programs written in a simple and intelligible form. This chapter describes the process of writing such programs in a language called BASIC. This language has proved so popular that nearly every computer has a translation program (such as a compiler) for it. On some microcomputers it is the only programming language available.

Before writing a program it is necessary to be clear about what the program is supposed to do. A trivial example is used here to keep the program simple. Let us suppose records are being kept of the number of eggs laid by a hen. Each week the number of eggs laid will be added to the total so far. A computer program is needed to add the number for the week to the previous total and produce the new total.

The BASIC language is designed for use from a keyboard terminal. Suppose there is such a terminal connected to a computer that can 'understand' BASIC. The previous total of eggs and the number for the week are to be typed at the terminal. The new total is to be displayed by the computer on the screen.

A tool which programmers sometimes use to clarify their thinking is *a flowchart*. This shows the sequence of operations in pictorial form, starting from a box marked START and ending at a box marked END. The flowchart for the egg-totalling program looks like this:

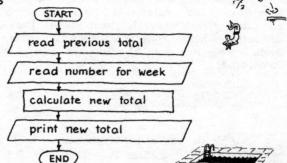

A program in BASIC may now be constructed from this flowchart. It is as follows:

This is very similar to the program on page 51 which was nearly a BASIC program. Both programs were designed to read two numbers, add them, then print the result. But the program on the right conforms to the rules of the BASIC language.

```
10  INPUT P
20  INPUT W
30  LET N = P + W
40  PRINT N
50  END
```

Statements in BASIC always begin with a number called the *line number*. This makes it possible to refer to any of the statements (as illustrated later in this chapter). It is customary to number the lines in tens.

The program on page 51 uses X, Y and Z to refer to words of main store holding numbers. These words of main store are called *variables* because their contents may vary during execution of the program. BASIC allows any single letter to be used as the name of a variable. Letters in this illustration have been chosen to remind us of the use of the variables: P for the previous total; W for the weekly number of eggs; N for the new total.

The END statement tells the BASIC compiler that there are no more BASIC statements to be translated. There must be an END as the last statement of every BASIC program.

The program shown above may be typed at the terminal. The statements then appear on the screen and are simultaneously sent down the wire to the computer where they are stored. After typing the whole program nothing happens until you type the command:

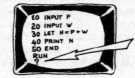

ruh

RUN

This is not a BASIC statement and so has no line number. It is a _command_ which tells the BASIC compiler to translate the program which has just been typed and then cause the translated program to be obeyed.

Because BASIC is designed for use from keyboard terminals, INPUT statements cause numbers to be read from the terminal and PRINT statements cause values to be displayed on the terminal. So the PRINT statement here has a different meaning from the one used in the last chapter which caused a number to be sent to a printer.

When the translated program is executed the first thing to happen is that the machine instructions corresponding to the BASIC statement number 10 are obeyed:

```
10   INPUT P
```

This requires a number (whose value is to be put into P) to be typed at the terminal. Some computers cause a question mark to be displayed on the terminal, then wait for the number to be typed.

```
10 INPUT P
20 INPUT W
30 LET N=P+W
40 PRINT N
50 END
RUN
?
```

INVITATION TO TYPE A NUMBER

As soon as the number has been typed the computer obeys the machine instructions corresponding to:

```
20 INPUT W
```

Once again a question mark appears on the screen and the computer waits for a number to be typed. When this has been done the two numbers are added together and the result displayed. The screen now looks like this:

Although this program works it is not necessarily easy for a poultry farmer to use. It is disconcerting to have the computer display a question mark and wait for a response. You may have no idea what item of data is needed. It would certainly be easier if the computer were to say what piece of information is required when asking for it. Because the computer does only what the program instructs it to do, the *program* must be changed so as to display the extra questions.

Before each of the two INPUT statements, PRINT statements may be inserted to cause the computer to display a message on the screen. The program then looks something like this:

The new PRINT statements are those with line numbers 5 and 15. The characters within the quotation marks are to be stored in the computer and displayed on the terminal when needed.

It is not necessary to retype the whole program. Apart from statements 5 and 15 the program is the same as before. The BASIC program typed earlier is still in the computer and can be added to or amended. All that is necessary is to type the two statements as shown above. These two statements are then added to the previous program. Their line numbers show where they fit in. This is why the original line numbers were in tens — so that additional statements could be inserted easily.

In order to see the program now held in the computer it is only necessary to type the command:

 List

In response to this the program is displayed on the screen.

```
LIST
5  PRINT "PREVIOUS TOTAL"
10 INPUT  P
15 PRINT "TOTAL FOR WEEK"
20 INPUT  W
30 LET  N = P + W
40 PRINT  N
50 END
```

Now when the command:

RUN

is typed, the amended program is translated and executed. The first message appears on the screen followed by the request for a number: ▷

```
PREVIOUS TOTAL
?
```

When this number is typed, the second message appears with another request for a number: ▷

```
PREVIOUS TOTAL
? 127
TOTAL FOR WEEK
?
```

When the second number is typed the result is displayed and the program stops:

```
PREVIOUS TOTAL
? 127
TOTAL FOR WEEK
? 15
142
```

Such a simple program is not very useful. It would be more useful if it could add several pairs of numbers because records are being kept for several hens. After calculating the new total for one hen the program should ask for the previous total for the next hen and so on. In other words the program should have a *loop* (see page 24). We should then need some way of ending the program. After the new total has been found for the last hen the program would continue to ask for another previous total. How can the program be informed there are no more totals? One way is by means of a negative number. A hen can never lay a negative number of eggs. The program could then test to see whether a negative number has been read. If it has, the program can be made to stop.

Here is a flowchart for this modied program:

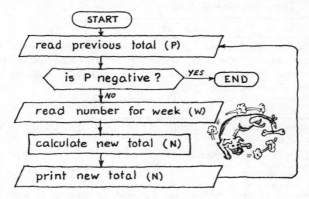

Boxes with pointed sides are used in a flowchart to show decision making. After a number has been read into P the value is tested to see if it is negative. Depending on the result of this test the program takes one of two routes; either to continue reading a value into W or to come to the end of execution. The 'YES' and 'NO' on the flowchart show which answers to the question cause that particular route to be taken.

If the value read into P is not negative a value is read into W, the new total is calculated and printed, then control returns to the beginning of the program to read a value into P once again.

Here is a BASIC program which corresponds to the above flowchart:

```
5    PRINT " PREVIOUS TOTAL"
10   INPUT  P
12   IF  P < 0  THEN  50
15   PRINT "TOTAL FOR WEEK"
20   INPUT  W
30   LET  N = P + W
40   PRINT  N
45   GO TO  5
50   END
```

The two new statements here need some explanation. The following line:

```
12   IF  P < 0   THEN  50
```

tests whether the value held in the variable called P is less than zero (that is, whether it is negative). If it is, then the next statement to be obeyed will be the one with line number 50:

```
50   END
```

which would cause the program to stop executing.

The line numbered 45:

```
45   GO TO 5
```

makes the next statement to be obeyed the one with line number 5:

```
5   PRINT  "PREVIOUS TOTAL"
```

at the start of the program. Line number 45 is translated into a machine instruction which changes the sequence register, just like the instruction at address 17 on page 23.

If the program shown on page 60 is still in the computer only the new lines (12 and 45) need to be typed.

Once again when the command **RUN** is typed the program is translated and executed. It now asks for pairs of numbers and totals them until a negative number is typed as a response to the question: PREVIOUS TOTAL? This causes the program to stop. A typical dialogue between a hen-keeper and the computer could look like this:

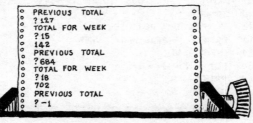

```
PREVIOUS TOTAL
? 127
TOTAL FOR WEEK
? 15
142
PREVIOUS TOTAL
? 684
TOTAL FOR WEEK
? 18
702
PREVIOUS TOTAL
? -1
```

⊙ne popular fallacy is that computers are likely to make mistakes. It does sometimes happen that the electronic circuitry goes wrong, but much less frequently than one might imagine. When it does happen the computer usually refuses to function at all until mended. What happens far more often is that *people* make mistakes. If there is a mistake in a program the computer may have no way of telling that the program is wrong. When the computer does what it has been told to do and faithfully obeys that program (perhaps printing a demand for a payment of nothing) newspaper reporters are keen to print the story that once again a computer has failed the human race. The story should be the other way round.

Let us suppose when typing line 45 for the program above there was a slip-up and the line ended up as:

```
45 GO TO 15
```

This could be because the programmer looked back to the wrong line or just made a mistake when typing. When the program is run a typical dialogue might look like this:

```
PREVIOUS TOTAL
? 127
TOTAL FOR WEEK
? 15
142
TOTAL  FOR WEEK
? 18
145
TOTAL  FOR WEEK
? -1
126
TOTAL  FOR WEEK
?
```

What *is* happening here? All goes well until the first result is displayed. The first number (127) has been read into P, the second number (15) into W and the result (142) is shown. Now instead of returning to line 5 to ask for another previous total, control passes to line 15 and another weekly total is requested. This value (18) is read into W. P still has its previous value of 127 so the result of the addition is 145 which is displayed on the screen. Once again control passes to line 15. This time —1 is typed to try to stop the program, but it doesn't work because the test for ending the run is at line 12. Drastic measures are needed to stop the program (such as switching off the computer).

Such a mistake in a program is known as *a bug*. (Bugs arise in programs because people make mistakes) Programmers not only write programs, they have to spend time *debugging* them — that is finding bugs and correcting them.

Programming can be a fascinating and absorbing occupation. Some people get hooked on it. You might like to study the program below and see if you can work out what it would do. The sign > means 'greater than'. In line 110 the message will first be printed and then the value of the variable on the same line.

```
10  PRINT "PLEASE TELL ME YOUR AGE"
20  INPUT  A
30  IF  A < 5  THEN  80
40  IF  A > 99  THEN  80
50  IF  A > 49  THEN  100
60  LET  X = A + A
70  GO TO  110
80  PRINT "I DON'T BELIEVE YOU"
90  GO TO  10
100 LET  X = A — 30
110 PRINT "YOU LOOK"; X
120 END
```

Those who want to learn more about programming are recommended to try *'Illustrating BASIC'* by Donald Alcock (Cambridge University Press, Cambridge, 1977).

10 WHO LOOKS AFTER THEM ?
(OPERATING SYSTEMS)

If a computer is likened to a car the programmer would be a bit like the one who sets the route. But doesn't it need a driver? Well, it does and it doesn't. It's rather a long story.

The story goes back to the time when computers were new. Not many people knew how to use them. Computers in those days were comparatively slow,

only doing a few thousand operations a second. If you worked in a place where there was a computer (perhaps a university or research establishment) and wanted to use it, you could book the computer for an hour or two. For that time the computer was all yours.

COMPUTER ROOM

KEEP OUT!
ITS MINE
UNTIL 3 PM
SIGNED
Programmer

The first thing you would do, perhaps, would be to read in a compiler program (see Chapter 8). This might be on a roll of paper tape kept in a drawer. It might take several minutes to put this tape through the paper-tape reader but this was no problem. There was plenty of time.

DRESS
c.1962

When the compiler had been read into the computer you would have to read in your own program for the compiler to translate. When your program was running that was the time to relax because the computer was fairly slow. Your program could be written in such a way that when it came to a crucial point the computer would type out a message and wait until you typed information directing the program which way to go.

That is the way things worked at the dawn of computers. It couldn't last. Before long computers were much faster and many more people felt they needed to use them. Personal sessions (where the programmer was both navigator and driver) were too wasteful of precious machine time. Another profession was created — the computer operator.

If you wanted to use the computer it was not so easy to book time to run the machine. The operator was now the chauffer and would only allow the programmer to take the wheel if it was vitally necessary. The usual way to use the computer was to hand over cards (or paper tapes) at a reception desk with a note to the operators telling them what compiler program was needed, what special needs your program might have when it was running, the time you expected it to take, and so on. This bundle handed in at reception was called a *job*. Operators would come out of the machine room at regular intervals to collect a batch of jobs which they would run on the computer one after another. This method of working was called *batch running*. When a batch of jobs was finished the output printed on the lineprinter would be brought out to reception for the programmers to collect.

No longer was it practicable to write programs that typed messages on a teletype and waited for a reply. With batch running everything had to be supplied with the deck of cards so that the operators did not have to mess around losing valuable time.

Computers became faster and ever more people wanted to use them. Instead of compilers being read from cards or paper tape they were read from magnetic tapes or disks — which are devices from which information can be read fastest.

Even with this improvement it was becoming clear that (the biggest delays in processing jobs were caused by human limitations of the operators) They had to select the appropriate compiler, read it in, start the compiled program running, stop the job if it overran its time. And their responses were no match for the speed of the new computers then emerging.

Then it was realised a program could undertake some of the operators' duties. The solution was a cleverly written program that stayed in the computer all the time and saw each job through — attending to its particular needs until the job was completed. The function of this special program was like the job of a travel agent who stays in the airport building all the time, shepherding each client on his way.

In the days when such programs were small and fairly simple these programs were called *monitors* or *supervisors*. Over the years they have become enormous and complicated. The name has also become more dignified; they are now referred to as *operating systems.*

With the operating system (often called 'the system') always resident in main store there was less room for compilers or the programs to be run. But storage was becoming progressively cheaper, therefore computers were given larger and larger memories.

Just as before it was necessary to enclose with each deck of cards a note telling the operators how the job was to be run, it was now necessary to give these details to the operating system. So the first cards of the deck had to be punched with information to tell the *operating system* who you were, how much time the job would take, which compiler you needed, and so on. This information was required so that the system could control the progress of the job. So the cards giving such information were called *job control cards*.

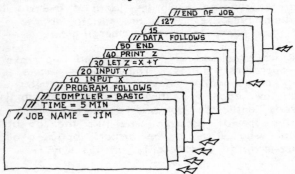

The job control cards would be read and acted upon by the system. In this example the BASIC compiler would be read into the main store and allowed to read and translate the program — perhaps putting the compiled program on a spare part of the magnetic disk. The operating system would then take over from the compiler, read the compiled program from its place on disk into main store, and allow this program to run, reading its data from cards and printing its results on the line printer.

Programs are now given 'permission' by the operating system to do their work. If a program runs too long the system steps in and kills it, then

allows the next job to run. As far as batch jobs
are concerned the operating system is Big Brother
— always watching.

It was possible to run more batch
jobs than previously. However, there
were still occasions when the computer *could* have done useful work
whilst waiting for other things to
happen. For instance, when a
program needs to read or punch a card, a fraction
of a second elapses before the peripheral can respond.
This time could have been spent in obeying thousands
of machine instructions.

On a golf course if one pair of players stops
for a chat or loses a ball in the rough, what
happens ? A player behind calls out to them
and another pair of golfers plays through. They,
in turn, may give way to other golfers before
reaching the nineteenth hole. The same sort of thing
can happen in a computer. If one program has to
wait another program can make use of the time by
having a chance to run.

This requires a more complicated operating
system. Such a system allows several jobs to have
programs inside the main store at the same time. The
system gives one program the go-ahead. When that
program has to wait for any reason the operating
system butts in and allows another program to run.
When this second program has to wait, the first program may not be needing to wait any more (for
instance, if it was waiting for a peripheral device
perhaps that device has now responded) so the operating system can set the first program running where

it left off. Now the second program has to wait.

Because there are (several programs executing by fits and starts at the same time) this is known as *multi-programming*. The operating system is much more complicated and therefore takes up yet more space. The rest of the main store has to be shared between the programs. But main store is getting progressively cheaper so computers are getting larger (in terms of memory capacity — not bulk).

There is a very important consequence of multi-programming. The computer can work efficiently even though one or more of the programs experiences long periods of waiting. Some peripheral devices are slower than others. (The slowest device of all is — a human being working at a keyboard terminal.) Because waiting time no longer matters programs can be written so as to display messages on terminals and wait for people to type replies. The wheel has gone full circle. Only this time every user may imagine he has the whole computer to himself. And the terminals do not need to be in the computer room; they can be in the programmers' offices.

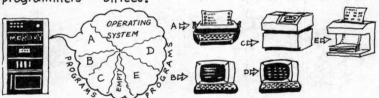

The picture above illustrates five programs running simultaneously in the computer under control of the operating system. Program A may be editing a file of data to correct some errors that have been found. Program B may be a trial version of a new program for calculating the cost of a mortgage. Program D may be one that plays space invaders. These three programs are being used from keyboard terminals. At the same time two batch jobs are running. Program C may be producing a statistical analysis of productivity and output over the last twelve months. Program E may be calculating and printing payslips for employees.

All these programs appear to execute at the same time. This is only possible because the operating system is so written that it can swop rapidly between different programs, ensuring none has to wait long before getting its turn to execute. This mode of working is often known as *time-sharing*.

What became of the operators? They are more necessary than ever. Although the operating system can now run the computer unaided for part of the time, there are many things a mere program cannot do - however cleverly written. Operators need to mount magnetic tapes on the tape drives. They have to fit a new box of paper on the line printer when it runs out. But besides these menial tasks they have to give the operating system instructions on how to do its work. An operator's job has thus become one requiring more skill as systems have become more complicated.

A new profession has meantime sprung into existence — the *systems programmer* — who devises and writes these complicated programs called operating systems.

The operating systems described in this chapter are those in use on large computers. However, even microcomputers now come with their own operating systems. These may be modest programs or they be complicated enough to permit one microcomputer to support several keyboard terminals at the same time.

THE HUMBLE
SYSTEMS
PROGRAMMER

11 WHAT USE ARE THEY ?
(APPLICATIONS)

    No one knows the full extent to which computers might be used. Every day new applications are found. There is space for only a few examples here to show the way in which computers are bringing about a revolution by subtle steps that often pass unnoticed.

    There are several reasons why computers are so useful. Because of the huge amounts spent on research computers are becoming more powerful, yet cheaper. Because computers are controlled by programs that are replaceable, computers may be adapted readily to new applications. The increasing variety of peripherals means that computers can interact with the outside world in many ways.

    Though there is no intrinsic difference between large and small computers (only differences in size, capacity, speed and cost) they tend to be used for very different purposes. This chapter deals only with medium to large computers — those that need a room to themselves. The next chapter describes how microcomputers are used.

    Everyone expects computers to excel at performing _calculations_. Some scientific research (in astronomy for instance) requires enormously complicated calculations to be performed. Were it not for high-speed computers much of this work would be too arduous to attempt. In some cases (for example weather forecasting) the problem requires not only enormous calculations but also speed. If the answer is late it is

"..AND TO EXPECT SOME THUNDER SOME TIME YESTERDAY MORNING.."

useless. Computers not only save people the drudgery of doing arithmetic, they do some things which would otherwise not be practicable.

Other jobs for which computers prove useful do not involve massive calculations but rather an enormous volume of clerical work; preparing electricity or telephone bills, for example, or printing wage slips. For each document produced there are a few details to be read (for example: basic wage, tax and other deductions) then a few simple calculations to be done. Then the results have to be printed on special stationery on a lineprinter. All this used to be done by hand; now it can be done more easily by computer — and with fewer mistakes.

To:
Usage of gass for the month of June 1898
×8-3-10-¾¾

Tasks like preparing accounts or wage slips involve only a little calculation but vast quantities of data have to be processed. Many reels of magnetic tape may be needed to store customers' names and addresses, account numbers and

so forth. Such applications are called _data processing_.

Data processing demonstrates that computers have another important asset besides an astonishing ability at arithmetic; they can cope with mountains of information. This leads to another kind of application for computers called _information retrieval._

A library may keep records of all its books on the disks of a computer. Then a librarian or reader may type at a terminal the hazy ideas he has about a book he wants to find. He may know, for instance, that it was written between 1930 and 1940, that the subject is geology and the word 'Recent' appears in the title. The computer then searches its records and displays details of all books that satisfy those conditions.

For information retrieval to be useful a large volume of information has to be available on a computer. Such a mass of information is called a _data base_. Every information-retrieval project is dependent on the accuracy and completeness of its data base. A bank may have a data base holding details of customers' accounts; a credit card company may record details of customer credit-worthiness; the police may have a data base of previous offenders (including digital records of their finger prints).

Computers can not only do arithmetic and handle large quantities of information; they can also _control_ things. For example computers are used in many cities to control traffic lights. Sensors in the road tell the computer the number of vehicles passing various key points. The computer then assesses where traffic is building up to a jam — and holds the lights longer at green to allow that traffic more time to flow through.

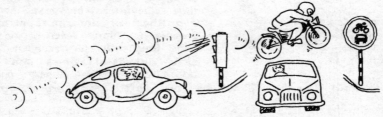

The sensors in the road are effectively another kind of input device to the computer which sends its output to the traffic lights.

Although it is impossible to classify applications of computers in any rigid way, these four aspects:

- _calculation_
- _data processing_
- _information retrieval_
- _control_

can be seen in the examples in this chapter.

Some supermarkets have increased efficiency and productivity by using *point-of-sale* terminals at each cash desk. The cashier does not have to type prices of articles into a cash register. Instead the cashier passes a 'wand' over a pattern of stripes printed on each wrapper. The items are automatically totalled and the amount displayed on the terminal. A receipt is printed and handed to the customer. This may contain not only the prices of things bought but also descriptions of them.

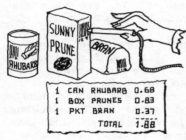

How is it done ? What looks like an ordinary cash register is in fact a peripheral device (the point-of-sale terminal) connected to a computer. The 'wand' converts the pattern of stripes into a product number which is sent to the computer. Using the product number the computer retrieves from its records a description of the item and its price. This information is sent back so that an itemized account can be printed by the point-of-sale terminal.

There are other things happening that you do not see. The computer now knows certain items have been sold then revises the count of how many items are in stock. If the number of a particular stock drops below a particular level the computer prints an order for a further delivery from the wholesaler. The management of the supermarket can readily discover what lines are selling fastest. All these benefits come from giving the cashier a point-of-sale terminal — which is also easier to use than a cash register.

Whereas a point-of-sale terminal brings the computer to the checkout desk, the next example brings the computer into the living room. An ordinary television receiver displays a picture twenty-five times every second.

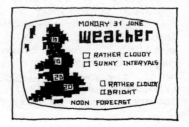

Each picture is made up of hundreds of lines. Some of the lines (such as those at the top of the picture) do not normally appear on the tube. The picture is spread so far that the top lines are lost. This gave someone an idea. Two lines at the top of every picture could be 'stolen' and used to transmit binary information. The receiver could be fitted with an extra piece of electronics to gather the bits and use them to display a static picture. By this means a viewer could at any time switch from a normal television channel to see a static page of news, weather forecast, share prices, *etc.*

Transmitting such binary information along ₂ ᵥᵢᵉʷᵈᵃᵗᵃ with a television signal is called *teletext*. Usually 100 pages of static information are transmitted at the rate of four pages a second. Besides a modified television receiver the viewer has a numeric key pad. When a number is keyed in the electronics cause the nominated page to be selected and displayed. The viewer may have to wait 25 seconds before that happens.

Computers are used to assemble and modify the pages to be displayed and fit the resulting teletext information into the television signal. But the idea has not ended with teletext.

Pages of information coded in binary are not confined to television channels. They can be transmitted via a cable such as a telephone line. The telephone company can provide a central service with access to a large number of pages. A factory may set up its own internal service with pages of regularly updated information to be consulted from terminals throughout the site or elsewhere. Sending binary pages of information along wires is known as *viewdata*. (Viewdata and teletext are together known as *videotex*.)

teletext

To receive viewdata information a television and special box of electronics are needed; alternatively a special viewdata terminal may be used.

Viewdata presents the viewer with his selected page much faster than teletext.

The terminal communicates with a computer which supplies the page within a fraction of a second. The computer operates in *time-sharing* mode (see page 71) and therefore can attend to many terminals simultaneously.

The pages of information may contain 'menus' – lists of *other* pages containing more detailed information. The number of one of these other pages may be typed on the keypad; the computer then retrieves and displays it. Also it is possible to send other information to the computer – not just the number of a page. For instance a page may display a numbered list of items of grocery. By typing a selection of these numbers the viewer may order a supply of groceries. This order is sent to the person to whom the original page of information belongs.

Viewdata is still in its infancy. Soon it may make computers accessible from many offices and homes.

Computers are used when making reservations (for airlines, theatres, hotels). When this was done without computers agents would telephone a central clerk stating their customers' needs. The clerk would note the reservation so as to avoid double bookings. The same procedure is followed when a computer is used, but now the computer takes over from the clerk; the agents use automatic terminals. Instead of a telephone conversation lasting several minutes (making other agents wait) the conversation

between terminal and
computer may be over
in a few seconds.
Whereas a clerk may
have difficulty answering
several telephones at
once this is no problem
to a computer.

...TO SIBERIA
RETURNING
2ND JUNE 1998

Computers are used in engineering in con-
junction with other equipment called *numerically-
controlled machines*. An engineering part may be
made from a piece of sheet metal or a casting.
This has to be drilled and machined in various
ways to produce the finished object. Various sizes
of drill and other tools have to be used at different
places and accurately positioned.

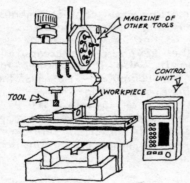

MAGAZINE OF
OTHER TOOLS

CONTROL
UNIT

TOOL

WORKPIECE

A numerically controlled
machine performs these
operations automatically
under control of a paper
tape or magnetic tape.
Tools are selected, fitted,
rotated, advanced and
withdrawn automatically
as required. At the same
time the workpiece is
accurately positioned on the
table so that each tool
is used at the right place.

How does the computer come into the picture?
The controlling tape for the numerically controlled
machine is produced on a computer. The sequence
of operations required is written in a special kind
of programming language. The computer (executing
a compiler program) translates this language into
instructions understood by the numerically controlled
machine. These instructions are coded on paper
tape or magnetic tape which is transferred from the
computer to the numerically controlled machine. This
whole operation is very similar to compiling a program
(see Chapter 8) — the only difference being that the
end product is in a form suitable for *another*

machine rather than the computer itself.

One area mentioned earlier in which the sheer calculating power of computers has been put to use is that of *weather forecasting*. The idea behind weather forecasting is that if full information about the current weather is available it is possible to work out what it will be, say, an hour from now. If the wind forces and directions are known, one can estimate how far the air will have moved in one direction. By then, of course, the winds may have changed in strength and direction as one air mass meets another travelling in a different direction with perhaps a different temperature, pressure and water content.

If the weather readings one hour from now can be calculated, the same can be done for the next hour, and the next, and so on. The more readings taken at the start — and the more calculations performed — the more accurate the forecast will be. There is just one crucial drawback. There is no value whatever in an accurate forecast for tomorrow if completed the day after tomorrow. The calculations must be done rapidly or not at all. It is not surprising that some of the largest and most powerful computers are used for weather forecasting.

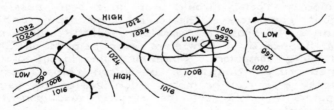

Another area where speed of calculation is all-important is that of *space flights*. Launching space satellites or rockets to the Moon would obviously be impossible without powerful rockets — but it would also be impossible without computers.

Accurate navigation is vital for space travel. Without it a satellite may be launched into an orbit which dips into the Earth's atmosphere. A flight to the Moon may need a mid-course correction or the spacecraft may miss the Moon altogether. Adjustments to the course are made by firing the rocket motors for carefully controlled periods. To know what correction is needed it is necessary to know the precise position, speed and direction of the spacecraft. Because the spacecraft is travelling at several kilometres per second these details must be established — and the required 'burn' calculated — as rapidly as possible. This is only one of many areas in which space flights demand the use of computers.

Many of the technical advances experienced in modern society would not have been possible without computers. The credit card boom and the advance towards a 'cashless society' could not have happened. Computers even help to design and build computers. Optimizing the layout of printed circuit boards or of silicon chips (see Chapter 6) can be made much easier by using computers to work out the simplest arrangement of components.

12 WHAT IS A MICRO ?

((MICROCOMPUTERS))

Space spectaculars and giant computers hit the headlines; tiny computers don't make such an impressive story. Yet it is the midgets that are beating the giants in transforming society. Because of the silicon chip (Chapter 6) it is now possible to make computers that are tiny yet possess great processing power. These are called *microcomputers*.

A silly extrapolation helps show the extent of miniaturization of computers. Suppose that in 1945 you bought a Rolls Royce and now wanted to replace it. If the same changes had happened to motor cars as have happened to computers your new Rolls Royce would now:

- cost as much as this book
- deliver 45,000 brake horse power
- do 3,000,000 miles to the gallon
- park six to a pin head

The term *micro* may be used for either a *microprocessor* or a *microcomputer*. A microprocessor may be described as a CPU on a chip. A CPU is not a complete computer; it needs store and peripherals to become one. A microcomputer is a computer built around a microprocessor.

Typically a microcomputer has a single printed circuit board with the microprocessor and about a dozen other chips containing store and circuitry to drive the peripherals. There must also be a power supply. There is a keyboard for input and a screen for output. All of these may be packaged into a piece of equipment looking like a VDU (see page 46).

MOST IMPORTANT
(SOME ARE NOT
EASY TO UNDERSTAND)

Sometimes in order to keep down costs a domestic television may be used as the output device on which the computer displays characters.

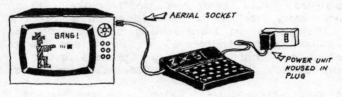

AERIAL SOCKET

POWER UNIT
HOUSED IN
PLUG

In addition there may be other peripherals attached to the microcomputer such as floppy disks (see page 48). Sometimes an ordinary cassette recorder is connected. These devices may be used to store programs or data.

Though a microcomputer may be smaller than a portable typewriter — and may cost as little — it is nevertheless a complete computer. It may be programmed to do what is wanted within the limits of its own hardware and the programmer's ingenuity. Usually manufacturers of microcomputers supply a program to translate BASIC so nobody need program a microcomputer in machine language. Programs can often be bought ready written and supplied on tape cassettes or floppy disks.

Microcomputers are so small and cheap they may be bought in a shop or by mail order (either complete or as a kit to be constructed). All kinds of people are discovering that computers provide an absorbing and amusing hobby. A *home computer* (or *personal computer*) can be programmed in one's spare time to calculate mortgage payments, keep track of income tax, remind one of appointments, suggest menus for meals — the list is endless. Those who do not want the amusement of writing programs may buy them ready written for simple business accounting and for playing a host of different games.

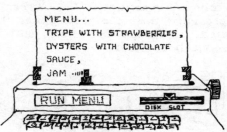

There is an array of glossy magazines for the computer hobbyist. Each month articles describe various facets of computing for the layman, including printed programs among which are usually some programs for new and ever more entertaining games.

Because micros have entered such a buoyant market through hobby shops there has been a tendency to dismiss them as toys for computer freaks. But they are not just toys. Though not as news-worthy, there are serious uses of microcomputers.

Leaders in the field of education realise the need for teaching children about computers. Until a few years ago the smallest computer was an enormous financial investment for a school. The best that could be done was to buy a keyboard terminal and connect it via a telephone line to a large computer, paying both for telephone charges and computer time. Now schools can buy their own microcomputers at a fraction of the cost.

A school computer may of course be used to teach children how to write programs (and some become very skilled at it). Programs already developed may be used for teaching other subjects — for instance how to spell. Backward children have been known to respond far better to a computer than to a teacher; the computer appears to have infinite patience. For the advanced student there are, for example, programs to simulate experiments in physics such as measuring the charge on an electron. The screen can be used to represent two charged plates between which charged oil drops are held stationary by varying the electric field.

Microcomputers can assist in running a business. The owner of a small business can buy a microcomputer and programs so that with little capital outlay he can enjoy some of the benefits computers have brought. Programs are available for accounting, payroll and stock control (keeping track of stock and reordering when necessary).

Doctors and dentists are using microcomputers for storing records of patients. Rather than searching through dog-eared files in massive cabinets, a record may be retrieved and displayed by computer in a split second. The record may easily be amended or extended by typing on the keyboard.

Mrs. Rica Gonda
The Manor.
Regular
patient.
Pays promptly.

DOG-EARED
FILE

Microcomputers — in place of large computers — are now controlling equipment or producing tapes for numerically controlled machines (see page 78).

In Chapter 2 a distinction is drawn between *special purpose* and *general purpose* computers. Because the program can readily be changed all computers so far described in this book have been general - purpose. But if you take a general purpose computer and run only *one* program on it then it becomes effectively special-purpose. It only does the one job defined by the single program.

Large computers are so expensive it is vital they be used as much as possible. Some are run twenty - four hours a day, seven days a week. To confine such machines to running just one program would be unthinkable — except, perhaps, for military defence systems.

A microcomputer is so cheap it does not need to be used all the time. Nor does it need to be used for all kinds of task. It can be used as the heart (perhaps 'brain' would be more correct) of a special piece of machinery built around it.

This is the case with popular game-playing machines. Such a machine plays games such as chess or backgammon, sensing its opponent's moves and indicating what move it is making in reply. There is usually a switch provided to control the level of play. The program stored in the micro takes the setting of this switch as one of its inputs. The higher the switch setting the more searching the program performs to find the best move.

CHECK MATE!

EFFECTIVE END GAME

The next example is far from being a toy. It provides an instance of the way computers are revolutionizing the working lives of many people.

There are few pieces of equipment used as widely as the office typewriter. In countless offices numberless secretaries type an endless stream of letters, reports and statements.

A good secretary can type accurately. A speed of 7 or 8 characters per second is considered very fast. If a mistake is made, however, there is a delay whilst the wrong character is painted over (or removed in some other way) and then retyped.

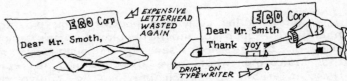

If a report is to be produced, a first draft may be typed and circulated to several people who comment on it. Then the whole report has to be retyped in amended form

> The future state ∧ of the economy of
> Outer Zoologica is ~~impossible~~ difficult to
> ~~ascertain~~ judge. It can only be said that

Some of the more expensive typewriters available give some help in correcting errors. (These machines are actually typewriters with a microprocessor to control them.) It is nevertheless a big step from sophisticated typewriter to *word processor.*

A typical word processor looks like a desk with a VDU on it and an automatic typewriter or printer beside it. Somewhere on the desk there may be floppy disk drives (see page 48).

The heart of the word processor is a micro-computer hidden in the desk. Its peripherals are the VDU, the printer and the floppy disks, each disk capable of holding large quantities of information.

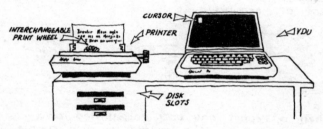

The typist types at the VDU. On the screen there is a cursor (a bright or flashing patch) which shows where the next character will fall. Words may be typed without regard to margins. If a word is started which runs off the end of a line —

> This is a line which will be excessi

— the microcomputer erases the word and places it on the next line before the typist has time to type another character. —

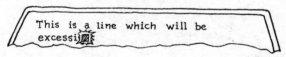

— This means the typist is able to type at full speed without worrying about coming to the end of a line. The computer takes care of that.

If a mistake is noticed on an earlier line buttons can be pressed to move the cursor back to this point. The misprint can then be retyped or letters deleted or extra letters inserted. Then by pressing buttons the cursor may be returned to the last line so that typing can continue.

After some material has been typed at the VDU it may be saved on part of a floppy disk for future reference. By pressing a button a copy of it may also be sent to the printer by the side of the desk. This will type the subject matter without any mistakes at a speed of 30 (or perhaps 45) characters per second.

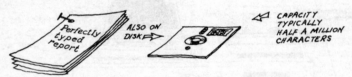

Perfectly typed report

ALSO ON DISK

CAPACITY TYPICALLY HALF A MILLION CHARACTERS

When a report has been circulated and amendments proposed the process is now simple. It is *not* necessary to re-type the whole report. The copy saved on floppy disk can be brought back a page at a time, corrections made, and the revised version saved on another part of the disk — to be printed as needed.

Letters that include standard common paragraphs may be produced with far less effort if those paragraphs are stored on disk to be retrieved and sent to the printer as part of a letter.

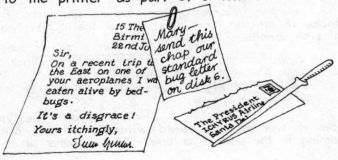

15 The
Birmi
22nd Ju
Sir,
On a recent trip t
the East on one of
your aeroplanes I wa
eaten alive by bed-
bugs.
It's a disgrace!
Yours itchingly,

Mary—
send this
chap our
standard
bug letter
on disk 6.

The President
ICHYRUS Airline
Santa Dei

Typed material usually has a straight left margin but the right-hand edge is 'ragged' because some lines are shorter than others. Printers for word processors are capable of spacing the words by varying amounts so that the right-hand margin is as neat as the left. The computer calculates how much space is needed and adjusts the spacing automatically.

Microprocessors are now at the heart of many pieces of equipment which would never be considered as computers. Some washing machines have a microprocessor (perhaps with a small amount of store on the chip) controlling the washing cycle for various materials. The input 'peripherals' would be sensors for the type of wash, water level and temperature. The output 'peripherals' would be the electric motor, the water supply, the water heater.

The program obeyed by the microprocessor lays down the sequence of events for the selected type of wash and checks continually that all is going according to plan. The microprocessor takes over the functions performed in older kinds of washing machine by specially designed cogs, cams, levers and electrical circuits.

WASHING-MACHINE REPAIR TEAM

HUMBLE PROGRAMMER   MECHANIC   ELECTRICIAN   PLUMBER

A microprocessor may be used to control the operation of a sewing machine, permitting far greater variety for special effects than is possible by means of extra appliances connected to the traditional machine.

Microprocessors are incorporated into some cars. They are used to minimize fuel consumption, monitor timing of the ignition, check the lights and run all the instruments on the dashboard.

Many computer peripherals (such as VDU's and lineprinters) have microprocessors inside to control them.

There is one kind of machine controlled by a microcomputer which is able to perform a wide variety of tasks. This is the *robot*. Unfortunately the popular idea of a robot is a mechanical man in shining armour. The robots used in industry consist of a flexible arm with a 'hand' at the end capable of gripping.

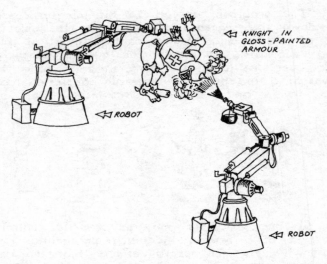

⟨◁ KNIGHT IN GLOSS-PAINTED ARMOUR

⟨◁ ROBOT

⟨◁ ROBOT

The microcomputer reads a series of instructions from a cassette tape and translates these into movements of the robot's joints. Alternatively the microcomputer can sense these movements and transform them into instructions for recording on cassette tape.

In order to 'program' the robot a human being literally takes it by the hand and leads it through the operations to be performed. For instance, spraying a complicated shape with paint is a task for a skilled spray-painter. Someone with experience is able to spray the surface with deft strokes so that an even coverage results with minimal use of paint. If such a painter clamps the spray gun in the hand of a robot and sprays one object, the robot will record all movements on tape and be able to repeat the operation exactly — as many times as necessary. The cassette tape that records the instructions for this operation may be removed from the robot's control unit and stored until needed again.

Robots are being used increasingly — not only for paint spraying but also for welding car bodies or loading work pieces on numerically controlled machines.

Many more examples could be given. The examples in this Chapter must suffice to show how computers — as they become progressively smaller — are pervading more facets of our lives; producing ever more rapid change.

13 WHERE WILL IT ALL LEAD ?
(FUTURE DEVELOPMENTS)

It is said that around 1947 International Business Machines (now world famous as IBM, the largest computer manufacturer) considered making computers and turned down the possibility. The reason (so the story goes) was that an estimated ten computers would be sold per year, and this one company could not be sure of selling more than six of these...

Forecasting what will happen with regard to computers is sure to make the crystal ball go misty.

ARIES, THE RAM

NEEDS ANOTHER 32K RAM

One thing is certain — things will *change*. Vast amounts of money are being poured into research and development; this investment is bound to retain the present climate of change.

⊙ne current trend is for chips to become progressively more complicated. The number of transistors that can be packed on one chip has almost doubled every year over the last two decades.

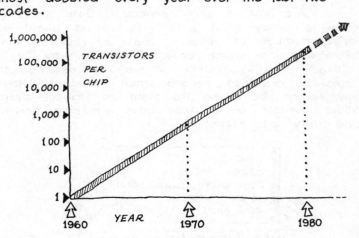

This trend means that electronic equipment of great complexity (such as a computer) is becoming steadily cheaper and more powerful. The basic components of electronics used to be transistors, resistors, capacitors. Now micro-processors and memories are becoming the fundamental components — with enormously greater potential but with each chip no more expensive than one of the old transistors.

As computer hardware becomes smaller, cheaper and more powerful, computer software does not keep pace. Writing programs is a skilled craft. Perhaps there will be a technical breakthrough enabling a programmer more easily to produce programs that are efficient, complete and free of bugs. For some years it has been prophesied that programming will become an obsolete profession — but there is still no sign of this happening.

Change is seldom welcomed. There are some aspects of the change brought about by computers that worry our society.

One fear is about *privacy*. Data bases (see page 74) may exist with information about a large number of people. That information may be wrong — in which case a person may be refused credit unfairly or may be assumed to have a criminal record when innocent. How can any person be given the right to inspect details about himself on a data base which is private and may be secret?

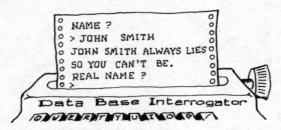

```
NAME ?
> JOHN SMITH
JOHN SMITH ALWAYS LIES
SO YOU CAN'T BE.
REAL NAME ?
>
```
Data Base Interrogator
QWERTYUIOP

Even if a data base holds accurate inform- ation there is the fear that computerizing such information makes it easier for it to fall into the wrong hands. True, doctors' records in a filing cabinet may be stolen, but when those records are stored in a computer they may be printed or copied rapidly leaving no trace of the theft.

...WASTE PAPER FOR OUR EMBASSY PLAYSCHOOL

COMPUTER BUREAU

One way of making confidential information more secure is by *encrypting* it. This means the characters are transformed in ways that make the words impossible to read (like spy codes). A computer program can be used to encrypt data or make the information legible again. But who is to look after this key program? It is just as vulnerable as the original data base.

Another fear concerns *responsibility*. Programming is done by many junior people but output produced by programs is accepted on trust by those in responsible positions. Structural engineers originally devised computer programs to analyse building frames to check that none of the imposed stresses exceeds safe limits. Today such programs do not stop at analysis; they produce a schedule of sizes for all beams, columns and slabs in the building. One such program was used to design industrial buildings — several of which were built before it was realized the program was *subtracting* rather than adding forces caused by wind. Just a minus sign in the wrong place. What if these buildings were nuclear power stations?

The Mariner 1 mission was to photograph Venus, but four minutes after blast off the spacecraft pitched into the Atlantic. The cause, again, was a misplaced minus sign in a computer program. This one cost about $ 10,000,000. Do any of the world's missile defence systems have misplaced minus signs?

The breakthrough in programming technique (referred to earlier) is impatiently awaited.

Another fear is that computers put people out of work. One computer (working tirelessly and accurately) does the same work as several people (needing coffee breaks and making mistakes). Therefore the computer gets the job and the people are put out of work. On the other hand if a company does not use the latest methods it will not be competitive, will therefore go out of business, and once again workpeople end up out of work.

The problems with computers resemble those of the time when mechanical looms were putting people out of work in the textile industry. Some workers – the Luddites – even smashed these new machines.

Nobody knows what the full effect of computers on industry might be. The pros and cons might be expressed as a dialogue:

 Computers have not put many people out of work yet.

No, but they are only just starting to be applied.

 Look at the industrial revolution – new jobs were created by it.

But this is a far more rapid change and more far-reaching.

 People will always be needed to design, program, manufacture and repair computers and electronic equipment.

 A company employing 100 people can make 5,000,000 chips a year — not many people will be needed.

 Just as machines were an addition to man's muscle power, so computers extend his brain power.

 That's just the reason why computers are replacing people in jobs formerly considered safe.

 Computers are necessary for industry to be efficient.

 What's the use of efficiency if unemployment continues to rise ?

 Well, if we don't use them our international competitors certainly will !

It may be that attitudes within society to such matters as full employment and working hours will have to undergo radical revision because of pressures from the computer revolution.

One might ask how the attitude of trade unions will affect the situation. Obviously the unions oppose redundancies and seek to cushion such effects on their members. On the other hand unions realise efficiency and productivity is in their interest also. A profitable concern employing a few people is able to pay higher wages. This can result in an increased standard of living for those at work while unemployment is rising. But the higher cost of labour may then persuade companies to automate still more — adding a further twist to the same spiral.

Unions have been known to threaten strike action *unless* robots were obtained to carry out hazardous or unpleasant tasks (like paint spraying). Unions have also discovered that industrial action can be effective if just the *computer* staff are called out. The other members may continue drawing pay as usual, but because of the vital importance of the computer the company is effectively crippled. (Terrorists, too, have not been slow to learn this lesson.)

FOR SECURITY REASONS
THIS ILLUSTRATION
WAS CENSORED

For good or ill computers are here to stay. They bring their problems, but so do many 'hopeless' adolescents who nevertheless grow up to be responsible and productive citizens.

When the history of the late twentieth century comes to be written this period will probably be classified not as the Nuclear Age, nor as the Plastics Age, nor even as the Space Age, but as the *Computer Age*.

INDEX

Ada 55
adding 20, 21, 22, 27–31
addresses 18 ff, 26, 27
Algol 55
analogue computers 8–9
AND–gate 30
APL 55
applications 72 ff
arithmetic 7, 10, 19, 31, 73
automation 96

BASIC 55, 56 ff, 82
batch running 66
binary digits, see bits
binary numbers 9, 10, 11 ff, 27 ff, 50 ff
bits 12, 18, 25 ff, 39
bugs 64, 93

calculation 8, 12, 16, 72
calculators 2, 7, 38
card reader 43
cards 43, 46
cassettes 82, 90–91
central processing unit, see CPU
chips, see silicon chips
Cobol 55
code 11
compilation 53–4
compilers 53 ff, 56, 78
computer
    control 74
    networks 49
    operators 66 ff
    revolution 3, 32, 72, 98

computers
    cost of 2–4, 32, 39, 82, 85
    digital 7–9
    general purpose 7–8, 85
    home 83
    number of 2, 32, 92
    personal 83
    physical appearance 6, 32, 81–2
    power to run 2, 32, 34, 39
    second generation 35
    special purpose 85
    speed of 22, 65, 72
    widespread use 1, 3
conditional transfer of control 24
conductors 32
control by computer 74
cores 12
CPU 18 ff, 27
credit cards 74

data bases 74, 94
data processing 73
debugging 64
digital computers 7–9
disk drive 47

electronics 3, 12, 24, 25 ff, 32 ff, 76, 93
engineering 78, 95
ENIAC 2

floppy disk drive 47–8
floppy disks 47–8, 82, 87–8
flowcharts 57, 61

Fortran 55.
full adder 31

gates 29 ff
general purpose computers
        7-8, 85
graphics terminals 48

half adder 28 ff
hardware 25 ff, 50, 93
home computers 83

industrial revolution 96
information retrieval 73-4
instructions 17, 18 ff, 50 ff
integers 13-14
integrated circuit 37

job control cards 68

keyboard terminals 45, 56 ff,
        70, 71
keypunch 43

languages, programming 51,
        55
lineprinter 45, 71
loops 24, 60
Luddites 96

machine instructions 18 ff,
        50 ff, 58
machine language 51
magnetic cores 12
magnetic disks 47
magnetic tapes 46, 71, 73, 78
main store 18 ff, 39
memory 7, 14, 18 ff, 68, 93
microcomputers 2, 5, 6, 39,
        48, 71, 81 ff
microelectronics 32 ff
microprocessors 38, 81, 93
micros, see microcomputers
microseconds 26
mini-computers 6
miniaturization 81
monitors 67
multi-programming 70

nanoseconds 26

networks 49
NOT-gate 30
numerical control 78, 85, 91

OCR readers 48
operating systems 5, 65 ff
operation code 20 ff
operators 66 ff
optical character recog-
        nition 48
OR-gate 29

paper tape 44-6, 78
paper tape punch 44
paper tape reader 44, 46
Pascal 55
peripherals 42 ff, 69-70, 72,
        75, 89
personal computers 83
photoresist 37
PL/1 55
plotters 48
point-of-sale terminals 75
printed circuits 35-6, 80
printers 45, 48, 87
privacy 94
program 4, 8, 10, 17, 20-4,
        50 ff, 56 ff, 65 ff, 95
programmers 8, 65-6, 71, 93, 95
programming 5, 56 ff, 95
programming languages 5,
        50 ff, 56 ff
punched cards 42-4, 46
punched paper tape 44-6

real numbers 14-15
registers 19 ff, 27
robots 90-91, 98

second-generation computers
        35
semiconductors 33
sequence register 23, 62
silicon 36-7
silicon chips 4, 7, 32 ff, 80,
        81, 93
Snobol 55
software 50, 93
space flights 8, 79-80, 95
special purpose computers 7-8, 85

speed of computers 22, 65, 72
store, main 18
supervisors 67
switches 26
system programmers 71

tape drive 46, 71
tape reader 44, 46
telephones 49
teletext 75-6
teletype 44, 45, 67
television 38, 75-6, 82
terminals 45, 56ff, 70, 73, 77
time sharing 71, 77
trade unions 98
transfer of control 24
transistors 35 ff, 93

translating a program 51 ff
typewriters 44-6, 86-9

unconditional transfer 24
unemployment 3, 96-8

vacuum tubes 33-4
variables 57
VDU 46, 47, 87
videotex 76
viewdata 76-7
visual display unit, see VDU

weather forecasting 73, 79
word length 18
word processors 86 ff
words 18 ff, 26 ff